THE COMPLL _ _
WOK
COOKBOOK

1000 Vibrant and Healthy Stir-fry Recipes for Both Beginners and Advanced Users

JASMINE POON

Table of Contents

Introduction

Chinese calling! Are you a Chinese food lover is ready to enjoy meals that you always order from your favorite restaurants? Look no further! We have dedicated our time and effort to understanding your needs and have prepared a lot of information and recipes that will walk you through the journey to enjoying your amazing delicacies. You can relax as we've got you covered. Ordering a Chinese dish is as easy as pressing a button, but what if I told you that it could even be easier with your wok at home? Interesting, right? The minutes you spend on your device trying to order something and then waiting for the delivery can be halved by making a decision to cook at home today. Not to mention that it would be cheaper too. Why should you make it difficult for yourself? Let us help you.

Chapter 1
Basics of Wok

What is a Wok?

A wok is a versatile cooking pot that originates from China. It is deep and has a round bottom. Although a wok is popular in other parts of the world, it's more common in China and other East and Southeast Asian countries. To answer the question of why you consider a wok to an ordinary pan- a wok distributes heat more evenly. It has either one or two handles. Amazingly enough, a wok was initially used to dry grains but was later used to prepare your favorite Stir-fryand more. How great! A wok is used for a variety of cooking methods. The methods include, but are not limited to, Stir Frying, steaming, pan frying, deep frying, braising, and poaching. A wok is indispensable for Chinese cooking. Pans and other pots are not comparable to a wok. This makes it a useful piece of equipment to have in your kitchen if you want to enjoy that Chinese meal from the comfort of your home. A wok is ideal for Stir Frying. It comes in various materials, with carbon steel being the best one.

Know your Wok

What wok meets your needs? This is an important aspect that we would like to help you understand. Please walk with us:

CARBON STEEL WOK

As the name suggests, this pot is made of carbon and iron. A carbon steel wok is a favorite for many chefs in the industry as it combines fast and even heating with durability. It could be your favorite today! Carbon steel woks do not have a non-stick coating. It develops naturally (after seasoning), which is non-toxic, unlike other non-stick coatings. These pots are:

- Lightweight
- Non-toxic
- Natural non-stick coating
- Even heating
- Durable

STAINLESS STEEL WOK

Stainless steel woks come in different types. Those that are coated and those that are not. If you bought an uncoated wok it's best to season it. Unlike carbon steel works, they are not naturally non-stick; therefore, use oil while cooking to avoid food sticking. Advantages:

- Durable
- Easy to clean
- Professional appearance
- Lightweight
- Requires very little maintenance

CAST IRON WOK

A cast iron wok is highly durable and holds heat longer, saving energy. The more you use this pot, the more it becomes non-stick. This means it doesn't lose its non-stick properties as it ages; instead, it improves. These are some of the advantages of using a cast iron wok:

- Durable
- Naturally non-stick finish
- Easy to use

ALUMINUM WOK

An aluminum wok provides the best heat distribution with a low heat capacity which means it will take longer to heat up. This wok is known for its heat conductivity, and if you want to make the best stir fries, this should be your choice. Unfortunately, an aluminum wok is not recommended for heavy cooking as it's softer than other materials.

Benefits of Using a Wok

HEALTHIER MEALS

Cooking in a wok involves less oil which means healthy eating with easy digestion. It also preserves the crispy texture of meat and vegetables, requiring less cooking time. Less cooking time limits nutrient loss such as vitamin C or B.

BETTER TASTING FOOD

Wok! What comes to your mind when you hear that? Woks are generally associated with better tasting food. It allows you to mix your food without changing the original flavors. Preparation is important as it enhances taste. Add your preferred ingredients and avoid overcooking.

EASY PREPARATION

A wok design ensures heat is distributed evenly, ensuring fast and effective cooking. This saves energy and cooking time. Mixed food is easy to prepare and cook as well, but your ingredients must be chopped evenly, cooked in small quantities of oil or sauce, and served as soon as it's ready.

BULK FOOD

One of the reasons why a wok is better than an ordinary pan is its ability to prepare larger quantities of food. You can prepare more of your favorite food to enjoy the next day. A wok is also better as it limits food spilling during cooking. Who doesn't want a clean kitchen?

LIMITED UTENSILS

A wok is a versatile piece of kitchen equipment. You can use it for different cooking methods, thus limiting the number of utensils when preparing a meal. Cleaning is easier as you don't use many utensils.

Pro Tips Of Using a Wok

- Get yourself the right wok. Pay attention to the design and material; is your wok round or flat bottomed? Make sure you get this right. If you are using a gas stove, get yourself a round bottomed one. Get a flat-bottomed one if you prefer an electric stove. You can also develop a non-stick coating that prevents food from sticking if you bought one without a coating. Carbon steel and cast-iron woks need to be seasoned, as do uncoated stainless-steel ones.
- Before first use, wash the wok in hot soapy water and rinse thoroughly, then dry with a soft cloth.
- Do not use metal utensils to avoid scratching off the non-stick coating.
- Prepare and slice your ingredients evenly. Wok cooking is all about preparation. Chop your ingredients as uniformly as possible to ensure proper cooking without scorching. You also do not want half-cooked, half-raw food.
- Use the right type of oil. This is an important consideration. Consider the type of food you are cooking, the kind of flavor you desire, and the preferred smoke point. Stir Frying, for example, requires oil with a high smoke point to prevent leaving your food with a bitter and burnt flavor. Consider using oils such as corn oil, soybean, and rice bran. Oils such as sesame oil are not recommended for high-heat cooking as they have a low smoke point.
- Do not overcrowd your wok. Overcrowding will leave your food soggy, hence missing the crispy texture. Be careful.
- Toss or flip your ingredients. You could use a spatula or any other equipment, but flipping is an important technique in using a wok, especially when cooking a stir fry, as speed is essential.
- Clean and take care of your wok after use as this ensures the wok lasts longer.

Chapter 2
Start your Wok Food Journey

Stir Frying

When you hear the word wok, you associate it with a stir fry. Do you know why? I will tell you, and it's because a wok excels in cooking a stir fry. Its shape makes it ideal for preparing a meal quickly and efficiently. The slopes make it easy to flip and toss the food, distributing heat evenly. To get that perfect stir fry, make sure you chop small uniform pieces. You can now enjoy your homemade chicken and vegetables Stir-fryin the comfort of your home. How convenient!

Steaming

Steaming is done using a kitchen appliance called a steamer. It is one of the oldest methods of Chinese cooking. The good news is that if you have a wok, you can steam your food by inserting a steam rack. Fill the wok with the appropriate water level, boil the water to get the steam going and then place the plate with your food on top of the rack. The benefits of this cooking method are that it is gentle and healthy. It doesn't involve the use of any oils. How does that sound? Great! Right? You might be tempted to start preparing your steamed fish but let's keep going to the end.

Pan-frying

With a wok, you can pan fry your food. This technique involves minimal oil or fat for cooking, unlike deep or shallow frying where you need a lot oil or fat. You will not need to lubricate the wok if you are cooking a greasy dish such as bacon. Before pan frying, you may consider covering your food with batter or breading it. We have prepared super easy pan-frying recipes that will help you enjoy tasty and healthy foods in the comfort of your home. Yummy!

Deep Frying

This is a cooking technique that involves submerging your food in hot oil. This method cooks food quickly and ensures that all the sides are cooked simultaneously. Most foods need a coating when deep frying; therefore, you can add that batter coating you like for protection. To avoid excessively greasy foods, prepare your food properly before emersion and fry it at the right temperature. The temperature depends on the type and thickness of the food. You can use a deep-fry thermometer to keep track of the temperature. It is also important to note that you shouldn't fill the oil more than halfway when using a wok to deep fry. Caution before anything else.

Braising

Braising is a cooking technique that involves both wet and dry heat cooking methods. The food is usually cooked at high temperatures and then simmered in the wok in cooking liquid. You could use any liquid of your preference, whether wine, coconut milk, or beer. Unlike stewing, braising requires less liquid and involves cooking larger pieces of meat. How does a red braised pork belly sound?

Poaching

This is a technique where food is heated while submerged in a liquid. Unlike simmering and boiling, poaching uses a lower temperature which is usually suitable for delicate foods. Too high a temperature will make the food fall apart and dry out. Some foods you can poach in a wok include, but not limited to, fish, fruit, poultry, and eggs.

Enjoy super easy recipes.

What makes us different is that we walk with you through the journey. We understand how hectic meal preparation can be, especially with a busy schedule and limited time, and therefore we want to help you create a reliable bond with your wok. Our recipes are easy to understand, use readily available ingredients with limited cooking time. Have your meal served in minutes. How great! Put on your apron and let's get to work.

If you are new here, we hope this introduction guides you to help understand where to start by understanding this Chinese kitchen master and providing easy recipes. We will hold your hand and walk with you step-by-step until you gain the confidence to try out recipes that suit your preference. Our aim is to provide you with information that makes working in your kitchen a pleasure and brings happiness to your home. You shouldn't miss a delicious Chinese dish by thinking you can only get it from your favorite Chinese restaurant. The time you've been waiting for has come. Enjoy!

Chapter 3
The Basics

Basic Steamed White Rice

Prep time: 5 minutes | Cook time: 35 minutes| Serves 4

- 2 cups rice
- 3 cups water

1. Rinse the rice in water until the water runs clear. Drain it and place it in a heavy-bottomed pot. Add the water.
2. Bring the water to a boil, uncovered. When it is boiling, stir the rice once, reduce the heat to a low simmer, and cover the pot with a lid.
3. Cook the rice for about 15 minutes, and then remove the covered pot from the heat. Do not uncover the pot. Let the rice rest in the covered pot for another 15 minutes to continue steaming.
4. Take off the lid, fluff the rice, and serve.

Chili Oil

Prep time: 5 minutes | Cook time: 3 hours| Makes 1½ cups

- 1 cup peanut oil
- ¼ cup sesame oil
- ½ cup crushed red chiles
- Chinese dried red chiles

1. In a small, heavy-bottomed saucepan, heat the peanut and sesame oils to about 250°F. Stir in the crushed red chiles. Turn off the heat immediately, and let the chiles steep in the oil for about 3 hours.
2. Strain the oil into a clean glass bottle. Store in the pantry or another cool, dark place.

Sesame with Spicy Chili Dip

Prep time: 5 minutes | Cook time: 0 minutes | Makes ¼ cup

- 4 tablespoons soy sauce
- 1 to 2 teaspoons Chinese chili sauce
- ½ teaspoon sesame oil

1. Whisk the ingredients together in a small bowl.

Soy and Vinegar Dipping Sauce

Prep time: 5 minutes| Makes ½ cup

- 3 tablespoons soy sauce
- 2 tablespoons Chinese black vinegar
- 1 teaspoon sesame oil

1. Whisk all the ingredients together in a small bowl.

Dumpling Wrappers

Prep time: 20 minutes| Makes about 50 wrappers

- 3 cups all-purpose flour
- 1½ cups room temperature water
- ½ teaspoon salt

1. In a large bowl, mix the flour, water, and salt. Transfer the dough to a work surface, lightly floured if necessary, and knead the dough until it becomes smooth.
2. Roll the dough into a cylinder, and cut it into about 30 pieces. Roll a dough piece into a small ball. Squash it down with your palm, and then use a rolling pin to roll it into a circular wrapper, about 3 inches in diameter.
3. The wrappers can be made in advance and frozen for up to three weeks. Lay the rolled-out wrappers, with pieces of parchment paper between them, in an airtight container.

Easy Ginger Chicken Broth

Prep time: 5 minutes | Cook time: 20 minutes| Makes 2 quarts

- 1 quart good-quality low-sodium chicken broth
- 1 cup water
- 1-inch piece of ginger, peeled and cut into thin pieces
- 3 cups Shaoxing rice wine

1. In a large pot, bring the broth, water, ginger, and rice wine to a boil.
2. Reduce the heat and simmer gently for about 20 minutes. Remove the ginger slices.

Sweet and Sour White Radish

Prep time: 40 minutes | Serves 4 as a side

- ½ large daikon radish, washed and peeled
- White vinegar, enough to cover the radish
- 6 tablespoons sugar

1. Cut the radish into thin, long strips. Place the strips in a large bowl, and cover them with the vinegar. Add the sugar and mix everything together to combine and dissolve the sugar. If necessary, use a heavy plate to keep the radish strips submerged. Let the radish sit for at least 20 minutes.
2. Serve immediately or store in your refrigerator.

Shredded Napa Cabbage Salad
Prep time: 20 minutes | Serves 4 as a side

- 1 tablespoon toasted sesame oil
- 1 tablespoon soy sauce
- 3 tablespoons rice vinegar or white vinegar
- 1 tablespoon sugar
- 3 cups finely shredded napa cabbage
- 1 cup shredded carrots
- 1 scallion, finely slivered

1. In a large bowl, whisk together the sesame oil, soy sauce, rice vinegar, and sugar.
2. Add the cabbage, carrots, and slivered scallion. Toss to combine.

Sriracha
Prep time: 10 minutes | Cook time: 10 minutes | Makes 1 cup

- 1½ pounds spicy red chile peppers, such as red jalapeño (hotter peppers make hotter sriracha)
- ½ cup apple cider vinegar
- 10 garlic cloves, finely minced
- ¼ cup tomato paste
- 1 tablespoon tamari or coconut aminos
- ½ teaspoon stevia
- 1 teaspoon sea salt

1. Stem, seed, and chop the chile peppers.
2. In a food processor or blender, combine all of the ingredients and purée until smooth.
3. In a small saucepan, bring the purée to a simmer over medium-high heat, and cook, stirring frequently, for about 10 minutes, until it's thick.
4. Store in a sterile container in the refrigerator for up to 1 month.

Sinangag
Prep time: 5 minutes | Cook time: 8 minutes | Serves 4

- 2 tablespoons cooking oil
- 8 cloves garlic, crushed and chopped
- 2 cups cold, cooked rice
- ¼ teaspoon kosher salt
- 4 scallions, cut into ¼-inch pieces

1. In a wok over medium-high heat, heat the cooking oil and garlic. Stir-fry for 2 minutes until the garlic turns golden brown but does not burn.
2. Remove half the garlic and reserve it for garnishing.
3. Gently sprinkle the rice and salt into the wok and Stir-fry for 1 minute.
4. Garnish with the chopped scallions and caramelized garlic before serving.

Egg Fried Rice (Chao Fan)
Prep time: 25 Minutes | Cook time: 5 Minutes | Serves 4

- 2 tablespoons cooking oil
- 2 garlic cloves, crushed and chopped
- 1 tablespoon crushed and chopped ginger
- 4 large eggs, scrambled
- 4 scallions, cut diagonally into ¼-inch pieces
- 2 cups cooked day-old rice
- ½ teaspoon salt
- ½ teaspoon black or white pepper
- 1 tablespoon soy sauce
- 1 teaspoon toasted sesame oil

1. In a wok, heat the cooking oil over high heat until it begins to smoke.
2. Add the garlic, ginger, and eggs to the wok and Stir-fry for 2 minutes, or until the eggs are cooked.
3. Add the scallions, rice, salt, pepper, soy sauce, and sesame oil and Stir-fry for 1 minute, or until all the ingredients are well combined, then serve.

Vegetable Chow Mein
Prep time: 25 Minutes | Cook time: 5 Minutes | Serves 4

- 8 ounces dried noodles
- 2 quarts water
- ¼ cup cooking oil
- 1 tablespoon crushed and chopped ginger
- 2 garlic cloves, crushed and chopped
- 1 medium onion, cut into 1-inch pieces
- 1 red bell pepper, cut into 1-inch pieces
- 24 sugar snap or snow pea pods, stemmed and strings removed
- ¼ cup hoisin sauce
- 4 scallions, cut into 1-inch pieces

1. Prepare the dried noodles by bringing the water to a rolling boil. Add the noodles to the pot and stir for 1 minute, until the noodles are flexible. Let them boil for 3 to 5 minutes, until the noodles are al dente, cooked but firm. Drain and set them aside.
2. In a wok, heat the cooking oil over high heat until it shimmers.
3. Place the cooked noodles in the wok and Stir-fry them for 2 minutes, until lightly browned.
4. Remove the noodles and all but 2 tablespoons oil and set aside.
5. Add the ginger, garlic, and onion to the wok and Stir-fry for 1 minute.
6. Add the bell pepper and pea pods to the wok and Stir-fry for 1 minute.
7. Return the noodles to the wok, along with the hoisin sauce, and Stir-fry for 1 minute.
8. Garnish with the scallions and serve.

Chapter 4
Sauces

Honeyed Chimichurri Sauce
Prep time: 15 minutes | Cook time: 0 minutes | Makes 1 cup

- 1 cup roughly chopped fresh cilantro
- 1 cup roughly chopped Italian parsley
- 4 sprigs fresh oregano
- 2 teaspoons minced garlic
- 1 serrano chili pepper, seeded and diced
- ½ tablespoon grated lime zest
- 2 tablespoons lime juice
- ¼ teaspoon red pepper flakes
- 1 tablespoon honey
- ½ cup olive oil
- ½ tablespoon kosher salt
- ¼ tablespoon black pepper

1. In a food processor or blender, add the cilantro, parsley, oregano, garlic, serrano chili, lime zest and juice, red pepper flakes, and honey. Pulse several times to break down the herbs.
2. Stream in the olive oil and blend until the items have fully incorporated. Season with salt and pepper to taste. Sauce can be stored in a sealed container in the refrigerator for up to 1 week.

Quick Garlicky Sriracha
Prep time: 10 minutes | Cook time: 10 minutes | Makes 1 cup

- 1½ pounds (680 g) spicy red chile peppers, such as red jalapeño (hotter peppers make hotter sriracha)
- ½ cup apple cider vinegar
- 10 garlic cloves, finely minced
- ¼ cup tomato paste
- 1 tablespoon tamari or coconut aminos
- ½ teaspoon stevia
- 1 teaspoon sea salt

1. Stem, seed, and chop the chile peppers.
2. In a food processor or blender, combine all of the ingredients and purée until smooth.
3. In a small saucepan, bring the purée to a simmer over medium-high heat, and cook, stirring frequently, for about 10 minutes, until it's thick.
4. Store in a sterile container in the refrigerator for up to 1 month.

Kung Pao Sauce
Prep time: 5 minutes| Makes 1¼ cups

- ¾ cup low-sodium chicken broth
- 3 tablespoons soy sauce
- 2½ tablespoons Shaoxing rice wine
- 1½ tablespoons Chinese black vinegar
- 1 teaspoon toasted sesame oil
- 2 teaspoons cornstarch

1. Whisk the ingredients together in a small bowl.
2. Use immediately or store in a glass jar in your refrigerator.

Easy Classic Stir-fry Sauce
Prep time: 10 minutes | Cook time: 0 minutes | Makes ½ cup

- 3 tablespoons soy sauce
- 3 tablespoons water
- 1 tablespoon oyster sauce
- 2 teaspoons red wine vinegar
- 2 teaspoons granulated sugar
- 1 teaspoon garlic salt
- ¼ teaspoon black pepper

1. Combine all the ingredients in a small bowl. Add this simple sauce in the final stages of Stir Frying. If you like, thicken the sauce by adding 1 teaspoon of cornstarch dissolved in 4 teaspoons of water.
2. Add the cornstarch and water mixture directly into the sauce in the wok or skillet, stirring quickly to thicken.

Scallion with Garlicky Black Bean Sauce
Prep time: 10 minutes | Cook time: 10 minutes | Makes 2 cups

- ½ cup fermented black beans
- 1 cup vegetable oil, divided
- 1 large shallot, finely minced
- 3 tablespoons peeled and minced fresh ginger
- 4 scallions, thinly sliced
- 6 garlic cloves, finely minced
- ½ cup Shaoxing rice wine

1. put the black beans in a small bowl, cover with hot water, and let soak for 10 minutes to soften. Drain and coarsely chop the beans.
2. Heat a wok over medium-high heat. Pour in ¼ cup of oil and swirl to coat the pan. Add the shallot, ginger, scallions, and garlic and Stir-fry for 1 minute, or until the mixture has softened.
3. Add the black beans and rice wine. Lower the heat to medium and cook for 3 to 4 minutes, until the mixture is reduced by half.
4. Transfer the mixture to an airtight container and cool to room temperature. Pour the remaining ¾ cup of oil over the top and cover tightly. Keep in the refrigerator until ready to use.
5. This fresh bean sauce will keep in the refrigerator in an airtight container for up to a month. If you wish to keep it for longer, freeze it in smaller portions.

Sesame Dipping Sauce
Prep time: 5 minutes| Makes ½ cup

- 4 tablespoons soy sauce
- 3 tablespoons rice wine vinegar
- 1 clove garlic, minced
- 1 tablespoon honey
- 1 teaspoon sesame oil
- 1 teaspoon sesame seeds

1. Whisk all the ingredients together in a small bowl.

Pepper and Orange Vinegary Sauce

Prep time: 10 minutes | Cook time: 0 minutes | Makes ⅔ cup

- 6 tablespoons orange juice
- 1 tablespoon fresh orange zest
- 2 tablespoons water
- 1 tablespoon rice vinegar
- 1 tablespoon dark soy sauce
- 2 teaspoons light soy sauce
- 2 teaspoons brown sugar
- ¼ teaspoon red pepper flakes

1. Combine the orange juice, zest, water, rice vinegar, dark soy sauce, light soy sauce, brown sugar, and red pepper flakes in a bowl. Either use immediately in a Stir-fry recipe or store in a sealed container in the refrigerator until ready to use. (Use the sauce within 3 or 4 days.)

Chili Sesame with Cornstarch Sauce

Prep time: 10 minutes | Cook time: 0 minutes | Makes ½ cup

- 4 tablespoons chicken broth
- 2 tablespoons red wine vinegar or Chinese red rice vinegar
- 2 tablespoons soy sauce
- 2 tablespoons sesame oil
- ½ tablespoon granulated sugar
- ¼ teaspoon chili paste
- 2 garlic cloves, finely minced
- 2 teaspoons cornstarch

1. Combine the chicken broth, vinegar, soy sauce, sesame oil, sugar, chili paste, and garlic in a bowl.
2. Whisk in the cornstarch. Either use the sauce immediately or store in a sealed container in the refrigerator until needed. (Use the sauce within 3 or 4 days.) Stir the sauce before adding to the Stir-fry to bring up any cornstarch that has settled on the bottom.

Brothy Kung Pao Sauce

Prep time: 10 minutes | Cook time: 0 minutes | Makes 1¼ cups

- ¾ cup low-sodium chicken broth
- 3 tablespoons soy sauce
- 2½ tablespoons Shaoxing rice wine
- 1½ tablespoons Chinese black vinegar
- 1 teaspoon toasted sesame oil
- 2 teaspoons cornstarch

1. Whisk the ingredients together in a small bowl. Use immediately or store in a glass jar in your refrigerator.

Sake with Gingered Teriyaki Sauce

Prep time: 10 minutes | Cook time: 8 minutes | Makes ¾ cup

- ¾ cup low-sodium soy sauce
- ½ cup water
- 1 tablespoon mirin
- 1 tablespoon sake
- 3 tablespoons light brown sugar
- ½ tablespoon minced garlic
- 1 tablespoon minced ginger

1. In a small saucepan over medium heat, whisk together all the ingredients and let the liquids come a low boil.
2. Reduce the heat to low and simmer the sauce until thickened, about 8 to 10 minutes. Use immediately or store covered in the refrigerator for 1 week.

Sugar with Vinegary Sauce

Prep time: 5 minutes | Cook time: 0 minutes | Makes 1 cup

- ¼ cup granulated sugar
- ¼ cup vinegar
- 2 tablespoons ketchup
- ¾ cup water
- 1 tablespoon cornstarch

1. Combine the sugar, vinegar, ketchup, and water in a medium bowl.
2. Whisk in the cornstarch. Use as called for in the Stir-fry recipe. Stir the sauce before adding to the Stir-fry to bring up any cornstarch that has settled on the bottom. If not using immediately, store the sauce in a sealed container in the refrigerator. (Use the sauce within 3 or 4 days.)

Buttered Sesame and Peanut Sauce

Prep time: 10 minutes | Cook time: 0 minutes | Makes 1½ cup

- 1 cup creamy peanut butter
- 1 tablespoon grated ginger
- 2 teaspoons sesame oil
- 1 tablespoon soy sauce
- 2 garlic cloves, minced
- 1 teaspoon red pepper flakes
- 2 tablespoons rice vinegar
- ¼ teaspoon kosher salt
- ¼ cup peanut oil

1. In a blender, add the peanut butter, ginger, sesame oil, soy sauce, garlic, red pepper flakes, rice vinegar, and salt. Blend until combined.
2. On the lowest setting, stream in the peanut oil until completely emulsified, approximately 2 to 3 minutes. Sauce should be used within the same day.

Soy Sauce with Chili Dip

Prep time: 5 minutes | Cook time: 0 minutes | Makes ¼ cup

- 4 tablespoons soy sauce
- 1 to 2 teaspoons Chinese chili sauce
- ½ teaspoon sesame oil

1. Whisk the ingredients together in a small bowl.

Classic Sesame and Stir-frySauce

Prep time: 10 minutes | Cook time: 0 minutes | Makes 1 cup

- ¼ cup low-sodium soy sauce
- ¼ cup oyster sauce
- 2 tablespoons Shaoxing wine
- 2 tablespoons honey or brown sugar
- 2 tablespoons water
- 1½ tablespoons sesame oil
- 1 tablespoon cornstarch
- 1 teaspoon chicken stock granules

1. Pinch ground white pepper.
2. Pour all the ingredients into a small jar or sealable container.
3. Shake until well combined.
4. Store in the refrigerator for up to 2 weeks.

Stocky Brown Sauce

Prep time: 5 minutes | Cook time: 0 minutes | Makes 1 cup

- 1 cup basic Chinese chicken stock, or store bought
- 2 tablespoons oyster sauce
- 1 tablespoon soy sauce
- 2 teaspoons cornstarch
- 1 teaspoon brown sugar
- ½ teaspoon sesame oil

1. Put all the ingredients in a small bowl and stir to combine. Stir well before using.
2. Alternatively, put all the ingredients in a small jar, seal, and gently shake to combine. Shake well before using.

Garlic with Honey Dipping Sauce

Prep time: 10 minutes | Cook time: 0 minutes | Makes ½ cup

- 4 tablespoons soy sauce
- 3 tablespoons rice wine vinegar
- 1 clove garlic, minced
- 1 tablespoon honey
- 1 teaspoon sesame oil
- 1 teaspoon sesame seeds

1. Whisk all the ingredients together in a small bowl.

Sesame and Vinegar Dipping Sauce

Prep time: 5 minutes | Cook time: 0 minutes | Makes ⅓ cup

- 3 tablespoons soy sauce
- 2 tablespoons Chinese black vinegar
- 1 teaspoon sesame oil

1. Whisk all the ingredients together in a small bowl.

Chinese Broccoli with Oyster Sauce

Prep time: 10 minutes | Cook time: 0 minutes | Serves 6 to 8

- 2 tablespoons peanut oil
- 4 garlic cloves, peeled and halved
- ½ (2-inch) piece ginger, peeled and julienned
- 1 pound (454 g) Chinese broccoli (kai lan), rinsed and cut into bite-size pieces
- 2 tablespoons oyster sauce
- 1 teaspoon sugar
- Pinch ground white pepper

1. In a wok over medium heat, heat the peanut oil.
2. Add the garlic. As soon as it starts to turn golden brown, add the ginger and give it all a quick stir.
3. Increase the heat to high and immediately add the kai lan, oyster sauce, sugar, and pepper.
4. Stir the kai lan well. Add a tablespoon or two of water to help steam it, if desired.
5. When the kai lan turns bright green and softens a little, remove it from the heat and serve immediately.

Limey Red Chili Sauce

Prep time: 5 minutes | Cook time: 0 minutes | Makes ¾ cup

- 6 fresh red chiles
- 2 garlic cloves, chopped
- 1 small shallot, thinly sliced
- 1 teaspoon freshly squeezed lime juice
- Pinch salt

1. Remove the seeds from the chiles, then cut the chiles into thin slices.
2. Put the sliced chiles, garlic, and shallot into a small blender or food processor. Blend for a few seconds or until it forms a paste. Alternatively, use a mortar and pestle to mash the ingredients.
3. Once the mixture is a paste, add the lime juice and salt. Stir to combine.

Vinegary Sauce with Ginger Mussels
Prep time: 10 minutes | Cook time: 5⅓ minutes | Serves 4 to 6

FOR THE SAUCE:
- 1 cup water
- 1 tablespoon black bean sauce
- 1 teaspoon rice vinegar
- 1 teaspoon sugar
- 1 teaspoon soy sauce
- ½ teaspoon dark soy sauce

FOR THE STIR FRY:
- 1 tablespoon peanut oil
- 2-inch piece ginger, peeled and julienned
- 2 garlic cloves, minced
- 2 pounds (907 g) fresh mussels, scrubbed and debearded
- 1 scallion, chopped into 1-inch pieces

1. In a small bowl, prepare the sauce by combining the water, black bean sauce, rice vinegar, sugar, soy sauce, and dark soy sauce. Set it aside.
2. In a wok over medium-high heat, heat the peanut oil.
3. Add the ginger and garlic and Stir-fry for about 20 seconds or until aromatic.
4. Add the mussels and sauce. Stir and reduce the heat to low.
5. Cover the wok for about 5 minutes, uncovering to stir the contents every minute or so.
6. When most of the shells have opened, turn off the heat and stir in the sesame oil and scallions. Discard any unopened mussels.
7. Transfer to a serving dish and serve immediately.

Plum Sauce
Prep time: 10 minutes | Cook time: 50 minutes | Makes 2 cup

- 4 cups coarsely chopped plums (about 1½ pounds)
- ½ small yellow onion, chopped
- ½-inch fresh ginger slice, peeled
- 1 garlic clove, peeled and smashed
- ½ cup water
- ⅓ cup light brown sugar
- ¼ cup apple cider vinegar
- ½ teaspoon Chinese five spice powder
- Kosher salt

1. In a wok, bring the plums, onion, ginger, garlic, and water to a boil over medium-high heat. Cover, reduce the heat to medium, and simmer, stirring occasionally, until the plums and onion are tender, about 20 minutes.
2. Transfer the mixture to a blender or food processor and blend until smooth. Return to the wok and stir in the sugar, vinegar, five spice powder, and a pinch of salt.
3. Turn the heat back to medium-high and bring to a boil, stirring frequently. Reduce the heat to low and simmer until the mixture reaches the consistency of applesauce, about 30 minutes.
4. Transfer to a clean jar and cool to room temperature. Refrigerate for up to a week or freeze for up to a month.

Chapter 5
Egg and Tofu

Salt and Black Pepper Tofu

Prep time: 5 minutes | Cook time: 5 minutes| Serves 4

TOFU BRINE

- 14 ounces firm tofu, sliced
- ¼ teaspoon garlic powder
- ½ teaspoon onion powder
- ½ teaspoon salt
- 1 teaspoon sugar
- 1¼ cups warm water
- ½ teaspoon sesame oil
- 1 teaspoon Shaoxing wine

TOFU SEASONING

- ¾ teaspoon salt
- ¾ teaspoon ground white pepper
- ¼ teaspoon ground Sichuan peppercorn
- ¼ teaspoon sand ginger powder
- 2 tablespoons all-purpose flour
- 2 tablespoons cornstarch

FOR THE DISH

- 4 tablespoons vegetable oil
- 5 garlic cloves, chopped
- 1 long hot green pepper, sliced
- 1 shallot, sliced
- 1 scallion, chopped
- 1 tablespoon cilantro, chopped

1. Mix tofu with all of its brine Prep time: 5 minutes | Cook time: 15 minutes| Serves 4in a bowl and cover to marinate for 2 hours.
2. Whisk flour with cornstarch, peppercorn, white pepper, salt, and ginger powder in a bowl.
3. To cook the tofu, heat oil in a Cantonese wok.
4. Dredge the marinated tofu through the flour mixture and sear in the wok until golden from both sides.
5. Serve warm.

Tofu Avocado Salad

Prep time: 5 minutes | Cook time: 5 minutes| Serves 4

- 7 ounces silken tofu, sliced
- 1 ripe avocado, peeled and sliced
- 2 garlic cloves, grated
- 1 teaspoon ginger, grated
- 2 tablespoons light soy sauce
- 1 teaspoon sesame oil
- ½ teaspoon sugar
- ½ teaspoon Chinese black vinegar
- ¼ teaspoon white pepper
- 2 teaspoons water
- Salt, to taste
- 1 scallion, finely chopped

1. Sauté tofu with sesame oil in a Mandarin wok for 5 minutes.
2. Toss tofu with rest of the salad in a salad bowl.
3. Mix well and serve.
4. Enjoy.

Brothy Cornstarch with Curried Tofu

Prep time: 15 minutes | Cook time: 6 minutes | Serves 4

- 2 tablespoons curry of choice
- 2 tablespoons rice vinegar
- 2 tablespoons soy sauce
- ½ cup vegetable or meat broth
- 2 tablespoons cornstarch
- 2 tablespoons cooking oil
- 2 garlic cloves, crushed and chopped
- 1 tablespoon crushed, chopped ginger
- 1 pound extra-firm tofu, well drained, patted dry, and cut into 1-inch pieces
- 1 medium carrot, roll-cut into ½-inch pieces
- 1 medium onion, cut into 1-inch pieces
- 4 ounces mushrooms, cut into slices
- 1 red bell pepper, cut into 1-inch pieces

1. In a small bowl, whisk together the curry, rice vinegar, soy sauce, broth, and cornstarch. Set aside.
2. In a wok over high heat, heat the cooking oil until it shimmers.
3. Add the garlic, ginger, and tofu and Stir-fryfor 2 minutes, or until the tofu begins to brown.
4. Add the carrot and Stir-fryfor 1 minute.
5. Add the onion and Stir-fryfor 1 minute.
6. Add the mushrooms and Stir-fryfor 1 minute.
7. Add the bell pepper and Stir-fryfor 1 minute.
8. Add the curry mixture to the wok and Stir-fryuntil a glaze forms.
9. Serve over basmati (Indian), coconut jasmine (Thai), or long-grain white rice (Chinese), depending on the type of curry you used.

Gingered Tofu

Prep time: 5 minutes | Cook time: 25 minutes| Serves 6

- 21 ounces firm tofu, cut into cubes
- 2 tablespoons oil
- 4 ginger slices
- 1 tablespoon Shaoxing wine
- 2 tablespoons Chinese black vinegar
- 3 tablespoons light soy sauce
- 4 tablespoons sugar
- 5 tablespoons water

1. Sauté ginger with oil in a Cantonese wok for 30 seconds.
2. Stir in tofu, and sauté for 10 minutes until it turns golden.
3. Add wine, black vinegar, soy sauce, water, and sugar.
4. Cover and cook for 15 minutes over medium low heat.
5. Serve warm.

Sesame Steamed Egg Custard

Prep time: 10 minutes | Cook time: 10 minutes | Serves 4

- 4 large eggs, at room temperature
- 1¾ cups low-sodium chicken broth or filtered water
- 2 teaspoons Shaoxing rice wine
- ½ teaspoon kosher salt
- 2 scallions, green part only, thinly sliced
- 4 teaspoons sesame oil

1. In a large bowl, whisk the eggs. Add the broth and rice wine and whisk to combine. Strain the egg mixture through a fine-mesh sieve set over a liquid measuring cup to remove air bubbles. Pour the egg mixture into 4 (6-ounce / 170-g) ramekins. With a paring knife, pop any bubbles on the surface of the egg mixture. Cover the ramekins with aluminum foil.
2. Rinse a bamboo steamer basket and its lid under cold water and place it in the wok. Pour in 2 inches of water, or until it comes above the bottom rim of the steamer by ¼ to ½ inch, but not so much that it touches the bottom of the basket. Place the ramekins in the steamer basket. Cover with the lid.
3. Bring the water to a boil, then reduce the heat to a low simmer. Steam over low heat for about 10 minutes or until the eggs are just set.
4. Carefully remove the ramekins from the steamer and garnish each custard with some scallions and a few drops of sesame oil. Serve immediately.

Chinese Tomato Egg Stir-fry

Prep time: 5 minutes | Cook time: 7 minutes | Serves 4

- 4 tomatoes, diced
- 1 scallion, chopped
- 4 eggs
- ¾ teaspoons salt
- ¼ teaspoon white pepper
- ½ teaspoon sesame oil
- 1 teaspoon Shaoxing wine
- 3 tablespoons vegetable oil
- 2 teaspoons sugar
- ¼–½ cup water

1. Sauté tomatoes and scallions with oil in a Cantonese wok for 2 minutes.
2. Beat eggs with salt, white pepper, sesame oil, wine, sugar, and water in a bowl.
3. Pour the eggs mixture into the wok and stir cook for 5 minutes.
4. Serve warm.

Kung Pao Tofu

Prep time: 5 minutes | Cook time: 6 minutes| Serves 6

TOFU

- 14 ounces firm tofu
- 1/3 cup cornstarch
- ¼ teaspoon garlic powder
- ¼ teaspoon onion powder
- 1/8 teaspoon five-spice powder
- ¼ teaspoon salt
- ¼ cup water

FOR THE REST

- 1 tablespoon soy sauce
- ½ teaspoon dark soy sauce
- 2 teaspoons sugar
- ¼ teaspoon salt
- 1 ½ teaspoon rice vinegar
- ½ teaspoon sesame oil
- 2 teaspoons cornstarch
- 2/3 cup warm water
- ¼ cup peanut oil
- 1 cup blanched peanuts
- 2 medium carrots chopped
- 1 tablespoon ginger, minced
- 3–5 dried chili peppers, chopped
- 3 garlic cloves, chopped
- 3 scallions, diced
- 1 teaspoon Sichuan peppercorn powder

1. For tofu, mix cornstarch with water, salt, five-spice powder, onion powder, and garlic powder in a bowl.
2. Mix soy sauces, sugar, salt, rice vinegar, cornstarch, sesame oil, and warm water in a bowl.
3. Sauté peanut with ¼ cup peanut oil in a Cantonese wok for 5 minutes, then transfer to a plate.
4. Sear the tofu in the same oil until golden-brown, then transfer to a plate.
5. Now sauté ginger and chili peppers with 1½ tablespoons peanut oil in a Cantonese wok for 1 minute.
6. Add tofu, peanuts, and prepared sauce.
7. Mix well and garnish with peppercorn.
8. Enjoy.

Braised Tofu
Prep time: 5 minutes | Cook time: 17 minutes| Serves 6

- 1 pound silken tofu
- 2 cups oil, for frying
- 1 cup chicken stock
- 1 tablespoon oyster sauce
- 1 ½ tablespoon soy sauce
- 1 teaspoon dark soy sauce
- ½ teaspoon sesame oil
- ¼ teaspoon sugar
- ¼ teaspoon salt
- 3 small ginger slices, 1/8 inch thick
- 3 garlic cloves, finely minced
- 2 scallions, chopped
- 4 fresh shiitake mushrooms
- 2/3 cup fresh winter bamboo shoots
- 1 tablespoon Shaoxing wine
- ½ cup snap peas
- 1 ½ tablespoon cornstarch

1. In a deep pan, heat 2 cups oil and deep fry the tofu until golden-brown.
2. Transfer the tofu to a plate and set it aside.
3. Sauté ginger with oil in a Cantonese wok for 15 seconds.
4. Stir in mushrooms, carrots, scallions, and bamboo shoots, and cook for 30 seconds.
5. Add snap peas, wine, all the sauces, sesame oil, sugar, and salt, then cook for 4 minutes
6. Mix cornstarch with water in a bowl and pour into the wok.
7. Stir and cook for 1–2 minutes until the mixture thickens.
8. Toss in deep fried tofu and mix well to coat.
9. Serve warm.

Tofu with Black Bean Sauce
Prep time: 5 minutes | Cook time: 15 minutes| Serves 4

- 1 pound firm tofu, diced
- 3 tablespoons oil
- 2 garlic cloves, minced
- 2 tablespoons fermented black beans, rinsed
- 2 scallions, whites and greens separated
- 3 dried red chilies, deseeded and chopped
- 1 tablespoon Shaoxing wine
- ½ tablespoon light soy sauce
- ½ teaspoon sesame oil
- ¼ teaspoon ground white pepper
- ¼ teaspoon sugar
- 1 teaspoon cornstarch, mixed with 2 tablespoons water

1. Sauté garlic with oil in a large wok for 30 seconds.
2. Stir in tofu and cook it for 5 minutes until golden-brown.
3. Add black beans, wine, soy sauce, red chillies, white pepper, sugar, and cover to a cook for 3 minutes.
4. Stir in cornstarch, mix well, and cook for 2 minutes.
5. Garnish with scallions.
6. Serve warm.

Chinese Tofu Salad
Prep time: 5 minutes | Cook time: 15 minutes| Serves 4

- 1 cup red bell pepper, julienned
- 1 cup red onion, sliced
- 1 cup carrot, julienned
- 1 cup cucumber, julienned
- 1 cup celery, julienned
- 8 ounces spiced tofu, shredded
- 1 tablespoon light olive oil
- 1 teaspoon garlic, minced
- 1 ½ teaspoons sugar
- ¼ teaspoon ground white pepper
- 2 tablespoons light soy sauce
- 1 tablespoon Chinese black vinegar
- 1 teaspoon sesame oil
- 1 tablespoon toasted sesame seeds
- ¼ cup cilantro, chopped

1. Sauté garlic, celery, carrot, onion, and bell pepper with oil in a Cantonese wok for 5 minutes.
2. Stir in tofu and sauté for 5 minutes.
3. Add soy sauce, white pepper, sugar, black vinegar, and cook for 5 minutes.
4. Remove it with from the heat and toss in cucumber.
5. Garnish with sesame seeds and cilantro.
6. Serve warm.

Tofu with Cashew Nuts Stir-fry
Prep time: 10 minutes | Cook time: 10 minutes | Serves 4

- 1/2 (340 g package of extra firm tofu (sliced
- 2 tablespoons of whiskey
- 1 tablespoon of fish sauce
- 1 tablespoon light soy sauce
- 1 tablespoon of black soy sauce
- 1 tablespoon of oyster sauce
- 2 tablespoons of vegetable oil or to taste
- 1 cup of unsalted raw cashew nuts
- 5 cloves of garlic, chopped
- 1 onion, cut into julienne
- 3 tablespoons of palm sugar
- 2 fresh red chili peppers (sliced)
- 3 tablespoons of water
- 4 green onions (sliced

1. Mix tofu, whiskey, fish sauce, light soy sauce, black soy sauce and oyster sauce in a bowl and marinate for 10 minutes. In the meantime, heat the oil in a wok over medium heat and let the cashews brown for 3 to 5 minutes.
2. Put cashew nuts in a bowl and pour out the oil. Put the garlic in the wok and Stir-fryfor 1 minute. Stir in tofu and onion and Stir-fryfor 1 minute.
3. Add the palm sugar and chili peppers. Fry for another 2 minutes. Add water and stir until everything is well mixed.
4. Take off the stove. Scatter cashew nuts and spring onions over the top.

Chinese Chives Eggs Stir-fry

Prep time: 5 minutes | Cook time: 7 minutes| Serves 6

- 5 large eggs
- 1/8 teaspoon sugar
- ½ teaspoon salt
- 1 teaspoon Shaoxing wine
- ¼ teaspoon ground white pepper
- ¼ teaspoon sesame oil
- 4 teaspoons water
- 2 cups Chinese chives, chopped
- 4 tablespoons vegetable oil

1. Beat eggs with sugar, salt, wine, white pepper, water, chives, and sesame oil in a bowl.
2. Set up a wok on medium heat and add vegetable oil to heat.
3. Pour the egg-wine mixture and Stir-fryfor 5–7 minutes until eggs are set.
4. Serve warm.

Curry Tofu Stir-fry

Prep time: 10 minutes | Cook time: 25 minutes | Serves 4

COOKING SPRAY

- 450 g extra firm tofu, cut into cubes
- 1 tablespoon of vegetable oil
- 1 cup of sliced fresh mushrooms
- 1 tablespoon of chopped garlic
- 3 cups of fresh spinach
- 2 tablespoons of soy sauce
- 1 1/2 tablespoons of curry powder
- 1 teaspoon red pepper flakes (optional)

1. Preheat the oven to 200 degrees C. Spray a baking sheet with baking spray; Arrange the tofu in one layer. Brown the tofu evenly in the preheated oven and turn over after 10 minutes for a total of approx. 20 minutes.
2. Heat vegetable oil in a wok or large pan over medium-high heat.
3. Add mushrooms and garlic; cook and stir until the mushrooms are soft; 2 to 3 minutes. Add tofu, spinach, soy sauce and curry powder; cook and stir until the spinach is wilted; 3 to 5 minutes. Scatter red pepper flakes over the mixture.

Egg with Garlicky Vegetables

Prep time: 10 minutes | Cook time: 1⅔ minutes | Serve 4

- 2 tablespoons cooking oil
- 3 garlic cloves, crushed and chopped
- 6 eggs, beaten
- 2 tablespoons rice wine
- 3 scallions, cut into ½-inch pieces
- 1 cup chopped bok choy
- 2 tablespoons soy sauce
- ¼ cup hoisin sauce

1. In a wok over high heat, heat the cooking oil until it shimmers.
2. Add the eggs and rice wine and Stir-fryuntil the eggs are firm but still moist.
3. Add the scallions and Stir-fryfor 30 seconds.
4. Add the bok choy and Stir-fryfor 1 minute.
5. In a small bowl, combine the soy sauce and hoisin sauce. Drizzle over the scrambled eggs. Serve alone or over steamed rice.

Vegetarian Tofu Stir-fry

Prep time: 10 minutes | Cook time: 10 minutes | Serves 2

- (1/4 cup frozen edamame without shell (green soybeans)
- 1/8 teaspoon salt
- 1 tablespoon of olive oil
- 1 clove of chopped garlic
- 1 cup of sliced yellow pepper
- 1/2 cup sliced yellow onion
- 1/2 cup bean sprouts
- 1 tablespoon of tamari soy sauce
- 2 cups of cooked pasta
- 1 tablespoon of sesame oil
- 1 teaspoon of roasted sesame seeds

1. Mix edamame and salt in a microwave-safe bowl; Cover and cook in the microwave for 1 minute. Heat the olive oil in a large wok over medium heat; Add garlic and cook until fragrant and sizzle, about 1 minute.
2. Add paprika and onion; cook and stir until they start to brown, about 2 minutes. Add bean sprouts and soy sauce; cook and stir until the soy sauce starts to evaporate, about 1 minute.
3. Add Edam, cooked noodles, sesame oil and sesame seeds; stir until the soy sauce starts to evaporate, about 30 seconds.

Chinese Steamed Eggs

Prep time: 5 minutes | Cook time: 25 minutes| Serves 4

- 3 medium eggs
- 2 teaspoons sea salt
- 1 cup water
- soy sauce
- sesame oil
- 1 scallion, finely chopped

1. In a large bowl, beat the eggs. Pour the eggs through a sieve into a steam-proof dish. Add the sea salt to the dish, and whisk it into the eggs.
2. In your wok over high heat, bring the water to a boil. Place a steamer rack or colander with legs in the wok. Carefully place the dish with the eggs in the wok, and cover the dish with a heat-proof plate. Turn the heat to low, and steam the eggs for 15 minutes.
3. Carefully remove the dish. Serve the eggs with soy sauce and sesame oil and garnished with a chopped scallion.

Vegetable Stir-fry with Tofu

Prep time: 10 minutes | Cook time: 10 minutes | Serves 4

- 6 tablespoons of olive oil
- 225 g firm tofu, drained well, cut into cubes
- 2 tablespoons of chopped, peeled, fresh ginger
- 3 cloves of garlic, chopped
- 450 g fresh shiitake mushrooms (stems trimmed and caps sliced)
- 2 cups of broccoli florets
- 2 red peppers, cut into strips
- 2 bunches of green onions, cut into pieces
- 1/2 cup sake or dry white wine
- 1/4 cup soy sauce
- 1 tablespoon of oriental sesame oil

1. Heat 3 tablespoons of olive oil in a large non-stick pan or Stir-fry over high heat. Add tofu; Stir gently until the edges start to brown, about 4 minutes.
2. Place in a bowl with a slotted spoon. Add 3 tablespoons of oil, ginger and garlic to the pan; Stir for 1 minute. Add mushrooms; Fry while stirring until they are soft and golden brown on the edge, approx. 5 minutes.
3. Add broccoli, paprika and spring onions; Fry while stirring until the vegetables are crispy and tender (approx. 3 minutes. Return the tofu to the pan; mix while stirring.
4. Stir in sake, soy sauce and sesame oil; Let simmer for 1 minute.
5. 5. Season with salt and pepper. Transfer to a large bowl and serve.

Tofu and Ripe Tomatoes Stir-fry

Prep time: 10 minutes | Cook time: 20 minutes | Serves 4

- 4 cups of rapeseed oil, for frying, plus 3 tablespoons
- 600 g medium or firm tofu, cut into cubes
- 1 cup sliced yellow onion
- 2 teaspoons of minced garlic
- 600 g of ripe tomatoes, cut into wedges
- 3 tablespoons mirin (rice wine)
- 1/2 cup green onions (cut into pieces)
- Salt, to taste

1. Heat 4 cups of rapeseed oil in a saucepan to 180 ° C. Fry the tofu cubes in portions until golden brown and make sure that they do not stick to each other.
2. Drain the tofu on paper towels. Heat a wok or large pan over high heat until hot. Add 3 tablespoons of canola oil.
3. Add onion and garlic and cook for 2 to 3 minutes while stirring. Add tomatoes and cook for 1 to 2 minutes, stirring carefully, until the tomatoes start to crumble.
4. Deglaze with mirin and cook for about 1 to 2 minutes.
5. Add tofu and spring onions, stir and season with salt.

Hot and Sour Vegetable Soup

Prep time: 5 minutes | Cook time: 25 minutes | Serves 4

- 4 cups chicken or vegetable broth
- 3 tablespoons soy sauce
- ¼ cup cooked shredded chicken (or pork)
- ½ cup shiitake or cremini mushrooms, diced
- 1 tablespoon garlic chili sauce
- ¼ cup white vinegar
- ¼ teaspoon ground pepper
- ⅓ cup canned bamboo shoots, julienned
- 3-ounce block of firm tofu, cut into ½-inch-thin strips
- 1 tablespoon cornstarch mixed with 1 tablespoon cold water
- 1 egg, beaten
- 2 scallions, diced
- ½ teaspoon toasted sesame oil

1. Bring the chicken broth to a simmer in your wok. Add the soy sauce, shredded chicken, shiitake mushrooms, and garlic chili sauce to the broth. Simmer for 3 to 5 minutes. Add the vinegar, pepper, bamboo shoots, and tofu to the wok. Simmer for 5 to 7 minutes more.
2. Add the cornstarch mixture to the soup, and stir the soup to combine. Simmer for about 5 minutes, until the soup has thickened.
3. Slowly pour the egg into the wok in a fine stream. Gently stir the soup a few times. Add the scallions and sesame oil to the soup. Give it a gentle stir and serve.

Broccoli and Tofu Stir-fry

Prep time: 5 minutes | Cook time: 25 minutes | Serves 4

- 1 tablespoon of peanut oil
- 4 cloves of garlic (chopped)
- 1 red pepper, deseeded and cut into strips
- 2 crowns of broccoli (cut into florets)
- 1/3 cup chicken broth
- 3 tablespoons of soy sauce
- 1 tablespoon of dry sherry
- 2 teaspoons of cornstarch
- 225 g extra firm tofu (diced)
- 2 tablespoons of cashew pieces

1. Heat peanut oil in a wok or large pan over a high temperature. Stir in the garlic and cook for a few seconds until it begins to brown. Add paprika and broccoli; Cook for about 5 minutes, until the peppers start to brown and soften.
2. Mix the chicken broth, soy sauce, sherry and cornstarch until they have dissolved. Pour the sauce into the wok and bring to a boil. Stir in the tofu and cook for about 1 minute until it is hot.
3. Garnish with cashew pieces to serve.

Pork Tofu with Watercress and Bean Sprouts
Prep time: 20 minutes | Cook time: 1 hour | Serves 8

- 900 g boneless pork loin, cut into strips
- 1 cup of soy sauce
- 3/4 cup of water
- 1 teaspoon of chopped fresh ginger root
- 1 tablespoon of coarsely ground black pepper
- 2 tufts of watercress ,dried, cut into lengths and thick stems discarded
- 225 gr. Bean sprouts
- 1 (450 gr. Package of firm tofu, drained and cut into cubes

1. Place pork in a wok or pan over medium heat. Cook and stir until the pork is browned on all sides, about 5 minutes. Stir in soy sauce, water, ginger and black pepper and bring to a boil over medium heat.
2. Reduce the heat to medium heat, cover and simmer, covered, until the meat is tender (approx. 40 minutes; Stir in the watercress and bean sprouts and continue to simmer until the meat is tender but still crispy (another 10 minutes.
3. Stir in the tofu, cover and simmer for another 5 minutes, approx. 10 minutes longer.

Class Egg Soup
Prep time: 5 minutes | Cook time: 15 minutes | Serves 4

- 6 cups chicken broth
- 1 teaspoon Shaoxing rice wine
- ¼ teaspoon ground ginger
- 1 teaspoon sugar
- ¼ teaspoon ground white pepper
- 1 tablespoon cornstarch, dissolved in 3 tablespoons water
- 2 large eggs
- Sea salt
- 1 scallion, green part only, thinly sliced

1. In your wok, mix together the chicken broth, rice wine, and ginger, and bring to a boil. Reduce the heat to a simmer, and stir in the sugar and white pepper. Stir the cornstarch mixture into the simmering soup, and continue simmering until the soup has thickened a bit.
2. In a small bowl, whisk the eggs lightly with a fork. Slowly stream the beaten egg into the soup, and keep gently stirring the soup while the egg is being added. The egg will form silky strands in the soup.
3. Turn off the heat immediately, and season the soup with the sea salt. Ladle the soup into individual bowls. Garnish with the thinly sliced scallion and serve.

Pasta with Fried Tofu Stir-fry
Prep time: 10 minutes | Cook time: 15 minutes | Serves 4

- 2 tablespoons of soy sauce and 2 tablespoons of tamari
- 3 tablespoons of hoisin or oyster sauce
- 1/4 cup broth or water
- 1 tablespoon rice wine or sherry
- 2 teaspoons of sugar and a little salt
- 1/4 cup coarsely chopped coriander plus long, sprigs for garnish
- 280 g package of Chinese egg noodles, cut wide
- 1 package of firm tofu (drained and cut into large cubes
- 2 1/2 tablespoons of roasted peanut oil
- 1 heaping tablespoon of chopped ginger and garlic
- 1 jalapeño chili (pitted and cut into cubes)
- 2 pieces of baked tofu, (thinly sliced
- 1 onion and 6 shiitake mushrooms, (thinly sliced
- 1 large broccoli, the head (cut into florets and sliced
- 1 red or yellow bell pepper (cut into narrow strips then halved
- 2 carrots (peeled and thinly sliced)
- 110 g kefen, cut and 1 bunch of spring onions, cut into lengths

1. Mix the sauce ingredients together and set aside. Bring a saucepan of water to a boil for the pasta and tofu. Reduce it to a boil, add the diced tofu and simmer on a low heat for 4 minutes. Lift out the tofu with a sieve and set aside.
2. Bring the water to the boil again, add the pasta and cook according to the instructions on the package. Drain and rinse under cold water. Mix with 1 tablespoon of oil and set aside and set up a wok or pan over high heat. Add the remaining oil and swirl around. When it's hot, add the ginger, garlic, chili, and baked tofu. Fry while stirring. When it's hot, add the ginger, garlic, chili, and baked tofu. Fry for 1 minute, stirring constantly, then add onion, mushrooms, broccoli, paprika and carrots.
3. Season to taste with a few pinches of salt and Stir-fry the vegetables for 3 minutes in the pan, then add the snow peas, spring onions and cooked tofu. Fry for another minute, stirring, then add the pasta and sauce. Reduce the heat, toggle it so that everything mixes evenly, cover and cook until the noodles are heated through - a matter of minutes. Turn out onto a large platter and garnish with sprigs of coriander.

Marbled Tea Eggs

Prep time: 5 minutes | Cook time: 2 hours | Serves 4

- 8 eggs
- 2 black tea bags
- ½ cup soy sauce
- 2 teaspoons sugar
- 2 pieces star anise
- 1 cinnamon stick
- 2 thin strips of orange peel

1. In a medium pot, cover the eggs with water. Bring the water to a boil, and then immediately turn the heat down to a simmer. Cook the eggs for about 10 minutes, until hard-boiled.
2. Remove the eggs from the pot, and cool them under cold running water.
3. Using the back of a spoon, crack the eggs evenly all around, making sure not to peel off the shells.
4. Return the eggs to the pot, and add the tea bags, soy sauce, sugar, star anise, cinnamon stick, and orange peel. Add enough water to the pot to cover the eggs.
5. Bring the water to a boil, and then immediately lower the heat. Simmer the eggs for 40 minutes. Turn off the heat, cover the pot with a lid, and then let the eggs steep for at least 1 hour. The longer you steep the eggs, the stronger the flavor and color will be.
6. Drain the eggs. Serve immediately as a snack or with noodles or rice.

Tomato and Egg Stir-fry

Prep time: 10 minutes | Cook time: 5 minutes | Serves 3

- 2 tablespoons of avocado oil, or as needed
- 6 eggs, beaten, 4 ripe tomatoes, cut into wedges
- 2 thinly sliced green onions

1. Heat 1 tablespoon of avocado oil in a wok or pan over medium heat. Boil eggs in the hot oil and stir until mostly cooked through, about 1 minute.
2. Transfer the eggs to a plate. Add 1 tablespoon of avocado oil to the wok and cook the tomatoes and stir until most of the liquid has evaporated, about 2 minutes.
3. Return the eggs to the wok and add the green onions; cook and stir until eggs are fully cooked, about 30 more seconds.

Lighter Egg Foo Young

Prep time: 5 minutes | Cook time: 15 minutes | Serves 4

FOR THE GRAVY

- ¾ cup chicken broth
- 1½ tablespoons hoisin sauce
- 1 tablespoon cornstarch dissolved in 2 tablespoons cold water
- For the egg foo young
- 3 to 3½ tablespoons peanut or vegetable oil, divided
- 3 or 4 shiitake or cremini mushrooms, thinly sliced
- 4 scallions, thinly sliced
- 1½ cups fresh bean sprouts
- ¼ cup chopped ham or Canadian bacon
- 1½ teaspoons soy sauce
- 1 teaspoon sesame oil
- 6 large eggs

1. Heat a wok over medium-high heat until a drop of water sizzles on contact. Add 1 tablespoon of peanut oil, and swirl to coat the bottom of the wok.
2. Add the shiitake mushrooms, scallions, and bean sprouts to the wok, and Stir-fry them for about 3 minutes. Add the ham, soy sauce, and sesame oil to the wok, and Stir-fry them for another 1 to 2 minutes. Remove the filling mixture from the wok and set it aside.
3. In a medium bowl, beat the eggs. Add the filling mixture to the eggs and mix to combine.
4. Heat the wok to medium-high, and add 1 tablespoon of peanut oil. Pour in one quarter of the egg mixture to make an omelet. Cook the egg mixture until it is golden brown, 1 to 2 minutes per side. Transfer the omelet to a plate. Repeat this step with the rest of the egg mixture to make a total of 4 omelets. For each subsequent omelet, use only 1½ teaspoons or less of the remaining peanut oil.
5. To serve, pour some gravy over each omelet.

Vinegary Tofu with Avocado Salad

Prep time: 10 minutes | Cook time: 5 minutes | Serves 4

- 7 ounces (198 g) silken tofu, sliced
- 1 ripe avocado, peeled and sliced
- 1 teaspoon ginger, grated
- 2 tablespoons light soy sauce
- 1 teaspoon sesame oil
- ½ teaspoon sugar
- ½ teaspoon Chinese black vinegar
- ¼ teaspoon white pepper
- 2 teaspoons water
- Salt, to taste
- 1 scallion, finely chopped

1. Sauté tofu with sesame oil in a Mandarin wok for 5 minutes.
2. Toss tofu with rest of the salad ingredients in a salad bowl.
3. Mix well and serve.
4. Enjoy.

Chapter 6
Poultry

Bok Choy, Chicken, Snow Peas and Mushrooms Stir -Fry
Prep time: 5 minutes | Cook time: 10 minutes| Serves 2

- 1/2 pound chicken
  1 cup sliced bok choy
- 1/2 cup snow peas
- 1/2 cup mushrooms
- 1 Tbsp. coconut oil

1. Marinade chicken in a Superfoods marinade. Stir-frydrained chicken and snow peas in coconut oil for 4-5 more minutes.
2. Add the rest of the marinade, mushrooms and Stir-fryfor a minute. Serve with brown rice or quinoa.

Chinese Cabbage, Chicken, Carrot and Leeks Stir -Fry
Prep time: 5 minutes | Cook time: 10 minutes| Serves 2

- 1 cup sliced Chinese cabbage
  1/2 pound chicken
- 1 cup shredded carrot
- 1/2 cup sliced leeks
- 1 Tbsp. oil

1. Marinade chicken in Superfoods marinade.
2. Stir-frydrained chicken in coconut oil for few minutes, add all vegetables and Stir-fryfor 2 more minutes.
3. Add the rest of the marinade and Stir-fryfor a minute.
4. Serve with brown rice or quinoa.

Chicken and Celery Stir-fry
Prep time: 5 minutes | Cook time: 10 minutes| Serves 2

- 1/2-pound chicken
  2 cups celery, diagonally sliced
- 1/2 cup sliced carrots
- 1 Tbsp. coconut oil

1. Marinade chicken in a Superfoods marinade.
2. Stir-frydrained chicken in coconut oil for few minutes, add all vegetables and Stir-fryfor 2 more minutes.
3. Add the rest of the marinade and Stir-fryfor a minute.
4. Serve with brown rice or quinoa over bed of lettuce.

Chicken, Peppers and Cashew Stir-fry
Prep time: 5 minutes | Cook time: 10 minutes| Serves 2

- 1/2-pound chicken
  1 cup red peppers
- 1 cup sliced green peppers
- 1/2 cup cashew
- 1 Tbsp. coconut oil

1. Marinade chicken in a Superfoods marinade.
2. Stir-frydrained chicken in coconut oil for few minutes, add all vegetables and cashew and Stir-fryfor 2 more minutes.
3. Add the rest of the marinade and Stir-fryfor a minute.
4. Serve with brown rice or quinoa.

Chicken, Broccoli and Cauliflower Stir-fry
Prep time: 5 minutes | Cook time: 10 minutes| Serves 2

- 1/2-pound chicken
  1 cup cauliflower
- 1/2 cup sliced carrots
- 1 cup broccoli
- 1 Tbsp. chopped onion
- 1 Tbsp. coconut oil

1. Marinade chicken in a Superfoods marinade.
2. Stir-frydrained chicken in coconut oil for few minutes, add all vegetables and Stir-fryfor 2 more minutes.
3. Add the rest of the marinade and Stir-fryfor a minute.
4. Serve with brown rice or quinoa.

Chickpeas, Zucchini and Chicken Stir-fry
Prep time: 5 minutes | Cook time: 10 minutes| Serves 2

- 1 cup sliced green zucchini
  1/2 pound cooked and drained chickpeas
- 1 cup sliced yellow zucchini
- 1/2 cup sliced onions
- 1 Tbsp. oil

1. Marinade chickpeas in Superfoods marinade.
2. Stir-frydrained chickpeas in coconut oil for few minutes, add all vegetables and Stir-fryfor 2 more minutes.
3. Add the rest of the marinade and Stir-fryfor a minute.
4. Serve with brown rice or quinoa.

Chicken Breast and Snow Peas Stir-fry
Prep time: 5 minutes | Cook time: 10 minutes| Serves 2

- 1/2-pound chicken breast
  2 cups snow peas
- 1/2 cup sliced red peppers
- 1/2 cup baby corn
- 1 Tbsp. coconut oil

1. Marinade chicken in a Superfoods marinade.
2. Stir-frydrained chicken in coconut oil for few minutes, add all vegetables and Stir-fryfor 2 more minutes.
3. Add the rest of the marinade and Stir-fryfor a minute.
4. Serve with brown rice or quinoa.

Snow Peas, Chicken and Asparagus Stir-fry
Prep time: 5 minutes | Cook time: 10 minutes| Serves 2

- 1/2 pound chicken
  2 cups sliced snow peas
- 1/2 cup sliced asparagus
- 1/2 cup julienned carrots
- 1 Tbsp. coconut oil

1. Marinade chicken in a Superfoods marinade.
2. Stir-frydrained chicken in coconut oil for few minutes, add all vegetables and Stir-fryfor 2 more minutes.
3. Add the rest of the marinade and Stir-fryfor a minute.
4. Serve with brown rice or quinoa.

Carrot, Leeks and Chicken Stir-fry
Prep time: 5 minutes | Cook time: 10 minutes| Serves 2

- 1/2 pound chicken
  1 + 1/2 cup sliced leeks
- 1 cup sliced carrots
- 1 Tbsp. coconut oil

1. Marinade chicken in a Superfoods marinade.
2. Stir-frydrained chicken in coconut oil for few minutes, add leeks and carrots and Stir-fryfor 2 more minutes.
3. Add the rest of the marinade and Stir-fryfor a minute.
4. Serve with brown rice or quinoa.

Chicken and Bok Choy Stir-fry
Prep time: 5 minutes | Cook time: 10 minutes| Serves 2

- 1/2 pound chicken
  2 cups sliced Bok Choy
- 1/4 cup sliced Chinese celery
- 1/2 cup sliced onions
- 1 Tbsp. coconut oil

1. Marinade chicken in a Superfoods marinade.
2. Stir-frydrained chicken in coconut oil for few minutes, add onions and Chinese celery and Stir-fryfor 2 more minutes.
3. Add the rest of the marinade and bok choy and Stir-fryfor a minute.
4. Serve with brown rice or quinoa.

Peking Duck with Bok Choy, Mushrooms, and Scallions
Prep time: 10 minutes | Cook time: 5 minutes | Serves 4

- 8 ounces boneless, skinless duck breasts, cut across the grain into ⅛-inch slices
- 1 tablespoon cornstarch
- 2 tablespoons Shaoxing rice wine
- 1 teaspoon five-spice powder
- 1 tablespoon soy sauce
- 2 tablespoons honey
- 1 teaspoon spicy sesame oil
- 2 tablespoons cooking oil
- 2 garlic cloves, crushed and chopped
- 1 tablespoon crushed and chopped peeled ginger
- 4 ounces mushrooms, sliced
- ¼ cup honey roasted peanuts
- ¼ cup hoisin sauce
- 2 cups diagonally sliced (½-inch) bok choy
- 4 scallions, green and white parts, cut diagonally into ¼-inch pieces

1. In a medium bowl, combine the duck, cornstarch, wine, five-spice powder, soy sauce, honey, and sesame oil. Mix well.
2. In a wok, heat the cooking oil over high heat until it begins to smoke.
3. Add the garlic, ginger, and duck. Stir-fryfor 1 minute, or until the garlic and ginger are fragrant.
4. Add the mushrooms, peanuts, and hoisin sauce. Stir-fryfor 1 minute, or until they are well combined with the other ingredients.
5. Add the bok choy and Stir-fryfor 1 minute, or until the leaves are bright green. The pale stalks will still be crisp.
6. Add the scallions and toss. Serve over rice or noodles.

Okra, Asparagus, Chicken and Onions Stir-fry

Prep time: 5 minutes | Cook time: 10 minutes| Serves 2

- 1/2 pound chicken
  1 cup sliced okra
- 1 cup sliced asparagus
- 1/2 cup sliced onions
- 1 Tbsp. coconut oil

1. Marinade chicken in a Korean Spicy marinade.
2. Stir-frydrained chicken in coconut oil for few minutes, add okra and asparagus and Stir-fryfor 2 more minutes.
3. Add the rest of the marinade and onions and Stir-fryfor a minute.
4. Serve with brown rice or quinoa.

Honey-Garlic Eggplant with Chicken

Prep time: 10 minutes | Cook time: 5 minutes | Serves 4

- 8 ounces boneless, skinless chicken thighs, cut across the grain into ⅛-inch pieces
- 1 tablespoon cornstarch
- 1 tablespoon Shaoxing rice wine
- 1 tablespoon soy sauce
- 1 teaspoon spicy sesame oil
- 2 tablespoons cooking oil
- 4 garlic cloves, crushed and chopped
- 1 tablespoon crushed and chopped peeled ginger
- 1 small eggplant, cut into ½-inch pieces
- 1 medium onion, cut into 1-inch pieces
- ¼ cup honey
- ¼ cup oyster sauce
- 4 scallions, green and white parts, cut diagonally into ¼-inch pieces
- Cooked rice or noodles, for serving

1. In a medium bowl, combine the chicken, cornstarch, wine, soy sauce, and sesame oil. Mix well.
2. In a wok, heat the cooking oil over high heat until it begins to smoke.
3. Add the garlic, ginger, and eggplant. Stir-fryfor 1 minute, or until the garlic and ginger are fragrant.
4. Add the chicken and Stir-fryfor 2 minutes, or until it begins to brown.
5. Add the onion and Stir-fryfor 1 minute, or until it is lightly coated with oil.
6. Add the honey and oyster sauce. Stir-fryfor 1 minute, or until the chicken and vegetables are coated with sauce.
7. Add the scallions and toss. Serve over rice or noodles.

Cashew Chicken with Bell Pepper and Bok Choy

Prep time: 10 minutes | Cook time:5 minutes | Serves 4

- 8 ounces boneless chicken thighs, cut across the grain into ⅛-inch pieces
- 1 tablespoon cornstarch
- 1 tablespoon Shaoxing rice wine
- 1 tablespoon soy sauce
- 1 teaspoon toasted sesame oil
- 2 tablespoons cooking oil
- 2 garlic cloves, crushed and chopped
- 1 tablespoon crushed and chopped peeled ginger
- 1 medium onion, diced into 1-inch pieces
- ½ cup whole salted cashews
- 1 large red bell pepper, diced into 1-inch pieces
- ¼ cup hoisin sauce
- 2 cups sliced bok choy (½-inch pieces cut across the grain, including leaves)
- 4 scallions, green and white parts, cut diagonally into ¼-inch pieces
- Cooked rice or noodles, for serving

1. In a medium bowl, combine the chicken, cornstarch, wine, soy sauce, and sesame oil. Mix well.
2. In a wok, heat the cooking oil over high heat until it begins to smoke.
3. Add the garlic, ginger, and chicken. Stir-fryfor 1 minute, or until the garlic and ginger are fragrant.
4. Add the onion and cashews. Stir-fryfor 1 minute, or until they are well combined with the other ingredients.
5. Add the bell pepper, hoisin sauce, and bok choy. Stir-fryfor 1 minute, or until the bok choy leaves are bright green. The pale stalks will still be crisp.
6. Add the scallions and toss. Serve over rice or noodles.

Sprouts, Broccoli, Red Peppers, Chicken and Cashew Stir-fry

Prep time: 5 minutes | Cook time: 10 minutes| Serves 2

- 1/2 pound cubed chicken
  1 cup sliced broccoli
- 1/2 cup sliced red peppers
- 1/2 cup cashews
- 1/2 cup sprouts
- 1 Tsp. coconut oil

1. Marinade chicken in a Superfoods marinade.
2. Stir-frydrained chicken in coconut oil for few minutes, add all vegetables and Stir-fryfor 2 more minutes.
3. Add the rest of the marinade and Stir-fryfor a minute.
4. Serve with brown rice or quinoa.

Sugar Snap Peas and Mushrooms with Five-Spice Chicken

Prep time: 10 minutes | Cook time: 5 minutes | Serves 4

- 8 ounces boneless chicken thighs, cut across the grain into ⅛-inch pieces
- 1 tablespoon cornstarch
- 2 tablespoons Shaoxing rice wine
- 2 tablespoons soy sauce
- 1 teaspoon five-spice powder
- 2 tablespoons cooking oil
- 2 garlic cloves, crushed and chopped
- 1 tablespoon crushed and chopped peeled ginger
- 1 medium onion, diced into 1-inch pieces
- 4 ounces shiitake mushrooms, sliced
- 2 dozen sugar snap pea pods
- 1 teaspoon spicy sesame oil
- ¼ cup oyster sauce
- 4 scallions, green and white parts, cut diagonally into ¼-inch pieces
- Cooked rice or noodles, for serving

1. In a medium bowl, combine the chicken, cornstarch, wine, soy sauce, and five-spice powder. Mix well.
2. In a wok, heat the cooking oil over high heat until it begins to smoke.
3. Add the garlic, ginger, and chicken. Stir-fry for 1 minute, or until the garlic and ginger are fragrant.
4. Add the onion and mushrooms. Stir-fry for 1 minute, or until the vegetables are lightly coated with oil.
5. Add the pea pods, sesame oil, and oyster sauce. Stir-fry for 1 minute, or until all of the ingredients are coated in the sauce.
6. Add the scallions and toss. Serve over rice or noodles.

Teriyaki Chicken with Napa Cabbage and Scallions

Prep time: 10 minutes | Cook time: 5 minutes | Serves 4

- 8 ounces boneless chicken thighs, cut across the grain into ⅛-inch pieces
- 1 tablespoon cornstarch
- 2 tablespoons mirin
- 1 tablespoon gluten-free tamari
- ¼ cup honey
- 1 teaspoon toasted sesame oil
- 2 tablespoons cooking oil
- 2 garlic cloves, crushed and chopped
- 1 tablespoon crushed and chopped peeled ginger
- 1 medium onion, diced into 1-inch pieces
- 1 red bell pepper, diced into 1-inch pieces
- 4 ounces shiitake mushrooms, sliced
- 1 cup diagonally sliced (1-inch) napa cabbage
- 4 scallions, green and white parts, cut diagonally into ¼-inch pieces
- Cooked rice or noodles, for serving

1. In a medium bowl, combine the chicken, cornstarch, mirin, tamari, honey, and sesame oil. Mix well.
2. In a wok, heat the cooking oil over high heat until it begins to smoke.
3. Add the garlic, ginger, and chicken. Stir-fry for 1 minute, or until the garlic and ginger are fragrant.
4. Add the onion, bell pepper, and mushrooms. Stir-fry for 1 minute, or until they are lightly coated with oil.
5. Add the cabbage and Stir-fry for 1 minute, or until well it is combined with the other ingredients.
6. Add the scallions and toss. Serve over rice or noodles.

Chicken, Mushrooms and Asparagus Stir-fry

Prep time: 5 minutes | Cook time: 10 minutes| Serves 2

- 1/2 pound chicken breast meat
  1 cups sliced asparagus
- 1/2 cup sliced carrot
- 1/2 cup sliced mushrooms
- 1 Tbsp. coconut oil

1. Marinade chicken in a Superfoods marinade.
2. Stir-fry drained chicken in coconut oil for few minutes, add all vegetables and Stir-fry for 2 more minutes.
3. Add the rest of the marinade and Stir-fry for a minute.
4. Serve with brown rice or quinoa.

Broccoli, Bell Pepper, and Mushrooms with Lemon-Pepper Chicken

Prep time: 10 minutes | Cook time: 5 minutes | Serves 4

- 8 ounces boneless chicken thighs, cut across the grain into ⅛-inch pieces
- 1 tablespoon cornstarch
- 2 tablespoons Shaoxing rice wine
- 1 tablespoon soy sauce
- 1 teaspoon freshly ground black pepper
- 2 tablespoons honey
- Juice of 1 lemon (2 tablespoons)
- 2 tablespoons cooking oil
- 2 garlic cloves, crushed and chopped
- 1 tablespoon crushed and chopped peeled ginger
- 2 cups broccoli florets
- Grated zest of 1 lemon (1 teaspoon)
- 4 ounces mushrooms, sliced
- 1 medium red or orange bell pepper, diced into 1-inch pieces
- 4 scallions, cut diagonally into ¼-inch pieces
- Cooked rice or noodles, for serving

1. In a medium bowl, combine the chicken, cornstarch, wine, soy sauce, black pepper, honey, and lemon juice. Mix well.
2. In a wok, heat the cooking oil over high heat until it begins to smoke.
3. Add the garlic, ginger, and chicken. Stir-fry for 1 minute, or until the garlic and ginger are fragrant.
4. Add the broccoli and lemon zest. Stir-fry for 1 minute, or until the broccoli is lightly coated with oil.
5. Add the mushrooms and bell pepper. Stir-fry for 1 minute, or until they are well combined with the other ingredients.
6. Add the scallions and toss. Serve over rice or noodles.

Sweet and Spicy Chicken with Peanuts and Lime

Prep time: 10 minutes | Cook time: 5 minutes | Serves 4

- 8 ounces boneless chicken thighs, cut across the grain into ⅛-inch pieces
- 1 tablespoon cornstarch
- 2 tablespoons Shaoxing rice wine
- 2 tablespoons soy sauce
- 2 tablespoons brown sugar
- 1 teaspoon spicy sesame oil
- Grated zest of 1 lime (1 teaspoon)
- 2 tablespoons cooking oil
- 2 garlic cloves, crushed and chopped
- 1 tablespoon crushed and chopped peeled ginger
- ½ teaspoon red pepper flakes
- 1 stalk of broccolini, sliced
- 1 red bell pepper, sliced
- 1 dozen green beans, cut into 2-inch pieces
- 4 bird's-eye chiles, cut into ½-inch pieces
- ½ cup honey roasted peanuts, coarsely chopped
- 4 scallions, green and white parts, cut diagonally into ¼-inch pieces
- 2 tablespoons Chinese black vinegar
- Juice of 1 lime (1 tablespoon)

1. In a medium bowl, combine the chicken, cornstarch, wine, soy sauce, sugar, sesame oil, and lime zest. Mix well.
2. In a wok, heat the cooking oil over high heat until it begins to smoke.
3. Add the garlic, ginger, red pepper flakes, and chicken. Stir-fry for 2 minutes, or until the chicken begins to brown.
4. Add the broccolini, bell pepper, green beans, and chiles. Stir-fry for 1 minute, or until they are lightly coated with oil.
5. Add the peanuts and Stir-fry for 1 minute, or until they are well combined with the other ingredients.
6. Add the scallions, vinegar, and lime juice. Stir-fry for 1 minute to combine. Serve over rice or noodles.

Cantonese Mushrooms and Bok Choy with Chicken

Prep time: 10 minutes | Cook time: 5 minutes | Serves 4

- 8 ounces boneless chicken thighs, cut across the grain into ⅛-inch pieces
- 1 tablespoon cornstarch
- 2 tablespoons Shaoxing rice wine
- 1 tablespoon soy sauce
- 1 teaspoon toasted sesame oil
- 2 tablespoons cooking oil
- 2 garlic cloves, crushed and chopped
- 1 tablespoon crushed and chopped peeled ginger
- 1 (15-ounce) can straw mushrooms, drained and rinsed
- 2 cups diagonally sliced (1-inch) bok choy
- ¼ cup oyster sauce
- 1 (8-ounce) can sliced water chestnuts, drained and rinsed
- 1 (8-ounce) can bamboo shoots, drained and rinsed
- 4 scallions, green and white parts, cut diagonally into ¼-inch pieces
- 1 tablespoon sesame seeds

1. In a medium bowl, combine the chicken, cornstarch, wine, soy sauce, and sesame oil. Mix well.
2. In a wok, heat the cooking oil over high heat until it begins to smoke.
3. Add the garlic, ginger, and chicken. Stir-fry for 2 minutes, or until the chicken begins to brown.
4. Add the mushrooms and bok choy. Stir-fry for 1 minute, or until the bok choy leaves are bright green. The pale stalks will still be crisp.
5. Add the oyster sauce, water chestnuts, and bamboo shoots. Stir-fry for 1 minute, or until all of the ingredients are coated in the sauce.
6. Toss with the scallions and sesame seeds and serve over rice or noodles.

Carrot and Chicken Curry

Prep time: 10 minutes | Cook time: 5 minutes | Serves 4

- 8 ounces boneless chicken thighs, cut across the grain into ⅛-inch pieces
- 1 tablespoon cornstarch
- 2 tablespoons Shaoxing rice wine
- 1 tablespoon curry powder
- 1 tablespoon soy sauce
- 1 teaspoon spicy sesame oil
- 2 tablespoons freshly squeezed lime juice
- ¼ cup ghee
- 1 garlic clove, crushed and chopped
- 1 tablespoon crushed and chopped peeled ginger
- 1 large carrot, roll-cut into ½-inch pieces
- 4 bird's-eye chiles, coarsely chopped
- 1 large onion, diced into 1-inch pieces
- Grated zest of 1 lime (1 teaspoon)
- 4 scallions, green and white parts, cut diagonally into ¼-inch pieces
- Cooked basmati rice, for serving

1. In a medium bowl, combine the chicken, cornstarch, wine, curry powder, soy sauce, sesame oil, and lime juice. Mix well.
2. In a wok, heat the ghee over high heat until it begins to smoke.
3. Add the garlic, ginger, carrot, and chicken. Stir-fry for 2 minutes, or until the chicken begins to brown.
4. Add the chiles, onion, and lime zest. Stir-fry for 1 minute, or until all of the ingredients are well combined.
5. Add the scallions and toss. Serve over basmati rice.

Thai Peppers and Peas with Chicken, Basil, and Mint

Prep time: 10 minutes | Cook time: 5 minutes | Serves 4

- 8 ounces boneless chicken thighs, cut across the grain into ⅛-inch pieces
- 1 tablespoon cornstarch
- 2 tablespoons Shaoxing rice wine
- 1 tablespoon soy sauce
- 1 teaspoon fish sauce
- Juice of 1 lime (1 tablespoon)
- 1 teaspoon spicy sesame oil
- 2 tablespoons coconut oil
- 2 garlic cloves, crushed and chopped
- 1 tablespoon crushed and chopped peeled ginger
- 6 bird's-eye chiles, coarsely chopped
- 2 cups sugar snap pea pods
- ¼ cup coarsely chopped fresh basil leaves
- ¼ cup coarsely chopped mint leaves
- 1 cup bean sprouts
- 4 scallions, green and white parts, cut diagonally into ¼-inch pieces
- Cooked jasmine rice or rice noodles, for serving

1. In a medium bowl, combine the chicken, cornstarch, wine, soy sauce, fish sauce, lime juice, and sesame oil. Mix well.
2. In a wok, heat the coconut oil until it begins to shimmer.
3. Add the garlic, ginger, and chicken. Stir-fry for 1 minute, or until the garlic and ginger are fragrant.
4. Add the chiles and Stir-fry for 1 minute, or until they are lightly coated with oil.
5. Add the pea pods and Stir-fry for 1 minute, or until they are bright green but still crisp.
6. Add the basil and mint. Stir-fry for 30 seconds, or until all of the ingredients are well combined.
7. Add the bean sprouts and scallions. Toss. Serve over jasmine rice or rice noodles.

Vietnamese-Style Broccoli, Carrot, and Baby Corn with Chicken and Lemongrass

Prep time: 10 minutes | Cook time: 5 minutes | Serves 4

- 8 ounces boneless chicken thighs, cut across the grain into ⅛-inch pieces
- 1 tablespoon cornstarch
- 2 tablespoons Shaoxing rice wine
- 1 teaspoon fish sauce
- Juice of 1 lime (1 tablespoon)
- 1 lemongrass stalk, peeled and minced
- 1 tablespoon brown sugar
- 1 tablespoon soy sauce
- 1 teaspoon spicy sesame oil
- 2 tablespoons coconut oil
- 2 garlic cloves, crushed and chopped
- 1 tablespoon crushed and chopped peeled ginger
- 1 medium carrot, roll-cut into ½-inch pieces
- 1 dozen small broccoli florets
- 1 tablespoon sweetened shredded coconut
- 1 (15-ounce) can baby corn, drained and rinsed
- ½ cup coarsely chopped cilantro
- 4 scallions, green and white parts, cut diagonally into ¼-inch pieces
- Cooked jasmine rice or rice noodles, for serving

1. In a medium bowl, combine the chicken, cornstarch, wine, fish sauce, lime juice, lemongrass, sugar, soy sauce, and sesame oil. Mix well.
2. In a wok, heat the coconut oil over high heat until it begins to shimmer.
3. Add the garlic, ginger, and chicken. Stir-fry for 1 minute, or until the garlic and ginger are fragrant.
4. Add the carrot and Stir-fry for 1 minute, or until it is lightly coated with oil.
5. Add the broccoli and coconut. Stir-fry for 1 minute, or until they are lightly coated with oil.
6. Add the baby corn and Stir-fry for 1 minute, or until all of the ingredients are well combined.
7. Add the cilantro and scallions. Toss. Serve over jasmine rice or rice noodles.

Butter Chicken with Black Bean Sauce, Potato, and Carrot

Prep time: 10 minutes | Cook time: 5 minutes | Serves 4

- 8 ounces boneless chicken thighs, cut across the grain into ⅛-inch pieces
- 1 tablespoon cornstarch
- 2 tablespoons Shaoxing rice wine
- 2 tablespoons soy sauce
- ¼ cup ghee
- 2 garlic cloves, crushed and chopped
- 1 tablespoon crushed and chopped peeled ginger
- 1 medium potato, julienned (1 cup)
- 1 large carrot, julienned (1 cup)
- ¼ cup black bean and garlic sauce
- 4 scallions, green and white parts, cut diagonally into ¼-inch pieces
- Cooked rice or noodles, for serving

1. In a medium bowl, combine the chicken, cornstarch, wine, and soy sauce. Mix well.
2. In a wok, heat the ghee over high heat until it begins to shimmer.
3. Add the garlic, ginger, and chicken. Stir-fry for 1 minute, or until the garlic and ginger are fragrant.
4. Add the potato and Stir-fry for 1 minute, or until it is lightly coated with oil.
5. Add the carrot and Stir-fry for 1 minute, or until it is lightly coated with oil.
6. Add the black bean sauce and Stir-fry for 1 minute, or until all of the ingredients are coated with the sauce.
7. Add the scallions and toss. Serve over rice or noodles.

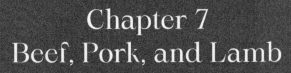

Chapter 7
Beef, Pork, and Lamb

Baby Corn, Bok Choy, Onion and Beef Stir Fry

Prep time: 5 minutes | Cook time: 10 minutes| Serves 2

- 1/2 pound beef stripes
  1 cup sliced bok choy
- 1/2 cup baby corn
- 1/2 cup onions
- 1 Tbsp. coconut oil

1. Marinade beef in a Superfoods marinade. Stir-frydrained beef and baby corn in coconut oil for 4-5 more minutes.
2. Add the rest of the marinade, onion and bok choy and Stir-fryfor a minute. Serve with brown rice or quinoa.

Beef, Carrot, Red Peppers and Green Onion Stir Fry

Prep time: 5 minutes | Cook time: 10 minutes| Serves 2

- 1 sliced carrot
  1/2 pound beef
- 1 cup sliced red peppers
- 1 cup sliced green onions
- 1 Tbsp. coconut oil

1. Marinade beef in a Superfoods marinade.
2. Stir-frydrained beef in coconut oil for few minutes, add all vegetables and Stir-fryfor 2 more minutes.
3. Add the rest of the marinade and Stir-fryfor a minute.
4. Serve with brown rice or quinoa.

Pork, Carrot and Onion Stir-fry

Prep time: 5 minutes | Cook time: 10 minutes| Serves 2

- 1 cup sliced carrot
  1/2 pound pork
- 1 cup sliced celery
- 1 cup sliced onions
- 1 Tbsp. coconut oil

1. Marinade pork in a Superfoods marinade.
2. Stir-frydrained pork in coconut oil for few minutes, add all vegetables and Stir-fryfor 2 more minutes.
3. Add the rest of the marinade and Stir-fryfor a minute. Serve with brown rice or quinoa.

Pepper Steak Stir-fry

Prep time: 5 minutes | Cook time: 10 minutes| Serves 2

- 1/2-pound steak
  1 cup red peppers
- 1/2 cup sliced green onions
- 1/2 cup sliced carrot
- 1 Tbsp. black pepper
- 1 Tbsp. coconut oil

1. Marinade steak in a Superfoods marinade and black pepper.
2. Stir-frydrained steak in coconut oil for few minutes, add all vegetables and Stir-fryfor 2 more minutes.
3. Add the rest of the marinade and Stir-fryfor a minute.
4. Serve with brown rice or quinoa.

Veal Szechuan Stir-fry

Prep time: 5 minutes | Cook time: 10 minutes| Serves 2

- 1/2-pound veal
  1/2 cup red peppers
- 1/2 cup sliced carrots
- 1/2 cup green peppers
- ½ cup onions
- 1 Tsp. Szechuan peppercorns, ground
- 1 Tsp. red pepper flakes
- 1 Tbsp. coconut oil

1. Marinade veal in a Superfoods marinade, Szechuan ground peppercorns and red pepper flakes.
2. Stir-frydrained veal in coconut oil for few minutes, add all vegetables and Stir-fryfor 2 more minutes.
3. Add the rest of the marinade and Stir-fryfor a minute.
4. Serve with brown rice or quinoa.

Leeks and Pork Fry

Prep time: 5 minutes | Cook time: 10 minutes| Serves 2

- 1/2 pound pork
  2 cups diagonally sliced leeks
- 1/2 cup celery
- 1 Tbsp. coconut oil

1. Marinade pork in a Superfoods marinade. Stir-frydrained pork and leeks in coconut oil for 4-5 more minutes.
2. Add the rest of the marinade, celery and Stir-fryfor a minute.
3. Serve with brown rice or quinoa.

Fish, Bok Choy, Onions and Tomato Stir-fry
Prep time: 5 minutes | Cook time: 10 minutes| Serves 2

- 1/2 pound fish filets (e.g. tilapia, cod, sole, flounder)
  1 cup sliced bok choy
- 1/2 cup tomato
- 1/2 cup onions
- 1 Tbsp. coconut oil

1. Marinade fish in a Superfoods marinade.
2. Stir-frydrained fish and onions in coconut oil for 4-5 more minutes.
3. Add the rest of the marinade, bok choy and tomato and Stir-fryfor a minute.
4. Serve with brown rice or quinoa.

Kale, Beef, Bok Choy and Green Garlic Stir-fry
Prep time: 5 minutes | Cook time: 10 minutes| Serves 2

- 1/2 pound beef
  1 cup sliced bok choy
- 1 cup sliced kale
- 1/2 cup sliced green garlic
- 1 Tbsp. coconut oil

1. Marinade beef in a Superfoods marinade.
2. Stir-frydrained beef, green garlic and kale in coconut oil for 4-5 more minutes.
3. Add the rest of the marinade, bok choy and Stir-fryfor a minute.
4. Serve with brown rice or quinoa.

Green Garlic, Pork, Ginger and Celery Stir-fry
Prep time: 5 minutes | Cook time: 10 minutes| Serves 2

- 1/2 pound pork
  1 cup sliced green garlic
- 1 Tbsp. minced ginger
- 1 cup celery
- 1 Tbsp. coconut oil

1. Marinade pork in a Superfoods marinade.
2. Stir-frydrained pork and green garlic in coconut oil for 4-5 more minutes.
3. Add the rest of the marinade, ginger and celery and Stir-fryfor a minute.
4. Serve with brown rice or quinoa.

Lamb, Broccoli, Mushrooms and Onions Stir-fry
Prep time: 5 minutes | Cook time: 10 minutes| Serves 2

- 1/2 pound lamb
  1 cup broccoli
- 1 cup mushrooms
- 1/2 cup onions
- 1 Tbsp. coconut oil

1. Marinade lamb in a Superfoods marinade.
2. Stir-frydrained lamb and broccoli in coconut oil for 4-5 more minutes.
3. Add the rest of the marinade, onions and mushrooms and Stir-fryfor a minute.
4. Serve with brown rice or quinoa.

String Beans, Onion and Beef Stir-fry
Prep time: 5 minutes | Cook time: 10 minutes| Serves 2

- 1/2 pound beef
  2 cups sliced string onion
- 1/2 cup sliced onions
- 1 red chili pepper
- 1 Tbsp. coconut oil

1. Marinade shrimp in a Superfoods marinade.
2. Stir-frydrained shrimp in coconut oil for few minutes, add all vegetables and Stir-fryfor 2 more minutes.
3. Add the rest of the marinade and Stir-fryfor a minute.
4. Serve with brown rice or quinoa.

Cabbage, Carrots, Pork and Almonds Stir-fry
Prep time: 5 minutes | Cook time: 10 minutes| Serves 2

- 1/2 pound pork
  2 cups sliced cabbage
- 1/4 cup sliced carrot
- 1/2 cup sliced onions
- 1 Tbsp. coconut oil
- 2 Tbsp. almonds

1. Marinade pork in a Superfoods marinade.
2. Stir-frydrained pork in coconut oil for few minutes, add onions, carrots, almonds and cabbage and Stir-fryfor 2 more minutes.
3. Add the rest of the marinade and Stir-fryfor a minute.
4. Serve with brown rice or quinoa.

Pork, Red Onions and Red Peppers Stir-fry

Prep time: 5 minutes | Cook time: 10 minutes| Serves 2

- 1/2 pound cubed pork
  1 cup sliced red peppers
- 1 cup sliced red onions
- 1 Tsp. coconut oil

1. Marinade pork in a Superfoods marinade.
2. Stir-frydrained pork in coconut oil for few minutes, add all vegetables and Stir-fryfor 2 more minutes.
3. Add the rest of the marinade and Stir-fryfor a minute.
4. Serve with brown rice or quinoa.

Lotus Root, Green Peas, Beef and Carrot Stir-fry

Prep time: 5 minutes | Cook time: 10 minutes| Serves 2

- 1/2 pound beef
  1 cup sliced lotus root
- 1/2 cup sliced carrot
- 1/2 cup sliced onions
- 1 Tbsp. coconut oil
- 1/2 green peas

1. Marinade beef in a Superfoods marinade.
2. Stir-frydrained beef in coconut oil for few minutes, add all veggies and Stir-fryfor 2 more minutes.
3. Add the rest of the marinade and Stir-fryfor a minute.
4. Serve with brown rice or quinoa.

Baby Corn, Beef and Ginger Stir-fry

Prep time: 5 minutes | Cook time: 10 minutes| Serves 2

- 1/2 pound beef
  2 cups baby corn
- 1 cup sliced onions
- 1 Tbsp. coconut oil
- 2 Tsp. minced ginger

1. Marinade beef in a Superfoods marinade.
2. Stir-frydrained beef in coconut oil for few minutes, add ginger, onions and baby corn and Stir-fryfor 2 more minutes.
3. Add the rest of the marinade and Stir-fryfor a minute.
4. Serve with brown rice or quinoa.

Beef, Bok Choy and Red Peppers Stir-fry

Prep time: 5 minutes | Cook time: 10 minutes| Serves 2

- 1/2 pound beef
  1 cup sliced bok choy
- 1/2 cup sliced cilantro
- 1/2 cup sliced onions
- 1 Tbsp. coconut oil
- 1/4 cup red peppers

1. Marinade beef in a Superfoods marinade.
2. Stir-frydrained beef in coconut oil for few minutes, add onions, bok choy and peppers and Stir-fryfor 2 more minutes.
3. Add the rest of the marinade and cilantro and Stir-fryfor a minute.
4. Serve with brown rice or quinoa.

Eggy Pork with Cornstarch

Prep time: 10 minutes | Cook time: 15 minutes | Serves 4 to 6

- ½ pound (227 g) ground pork
- 2 teaspoons soy sauce
- 1 teaspoon cornstarch
- ½ teaspoon salt
- Pinch freshly ground black pepper
- 3 eggs
- ½ cup water
- 1 teaspoon Shaoxing wine
- 2 teaspoons finely diced Chinese preserved radish (optional)

1. In a medium bowl, combine the ground pork, preserved radish (if using), soy sauce, cornstarch, salt, and pepper, mixing it well. Marinate at room temperature for about 15 minutes.
2. Set up a steaming rack in a wok, fill it with water halfway up to the rack, and set the heat to medium.
3. In a separate bowl, whisk the eggs with the water and Shaoxing wine. Set it aside.
4. Transfer the ground pork mixture to a shallow heatproof dish. Spread the ground pork in a single layer to cover the dish.
5. Pour the egg mixture evenly over the ground pork.
6. Cover the dish with aluminum foil. This will prevent water from dripping onto the custard.
7. When the water in the wok starts to boil, place the dish on the steaming rack.
8. Steam for about 15 minutes or until the custard is set, then serve.

Spicy Ketchup with Pork Ribs

Prep time: 15 minutes | Cook time: 6 minutes | Serves 4 to 6

FOR THE MARINADE:

- 2 teaspoons Chinese rose wine
- 2 pounds (907 g) pork ribs, cut into about 1½-inch pieces
- ½ teaspoon salt
- Pinch ground white pepper
- ¼ teaspoon five-spice powder
- 3 teaspoons cornstarch

FOR THE SAUCE:

- 2 tablespoons ketchup
- 1½ tablespoons apple cider vinegar
- 2 teaspoons brown sugar
- 1 teaspoon soy sauce
- ½ teaspoon dark soy sauce
- Pinch five-spice powder

FOR THE STIR FRY:

- 2 tablespoons peanut oil
- 2 garlic cloves, minced

1. Pour the Chinese rose wine over the pork. Add the salt, pepper, and five-spice powder. Mix well, then coat the pork with the cornstarch. Marinate at room temperature for 20 minutes.
2. In a small bowl, prepare the sauce by mixing together the ketchup, apple cider vinegar, brown sugar, soy sauce, dark soy sauce, and five-spice powder.
3. In a wok over medium-high heat, heat the peanut oil.
4. Arrange the pork ribs in the wok in a single layer. Cook without stirring for about 30 seconds, reduce the heat to medium, and Stir-fry for about 5 minutes or until the pork is cooked and golden brown.
5. Add the garlic and Stir-fry for about 20 seconds until aromatic.
6. Stir in the sauce, coating the ribs.
7. Transfer the ribs and sauce to a serving plate.

Spiced Pork Ribs in Soy Sauce

Prep time: 15 minutes | Cook time: 23 minutes | Serves 4 to 6

FOR THE MARINADE:

- 2 teaspoons Shaoxing wine
- 2 teaspoons cornstarch
- ½ teaspoon salt
- Pinch ground white pepper
- 2 pounds (907 g) pork ribs, cut into 1½-inch pieces

FOR THE SAUCE:

- 1½ cups water
- 2 tablespoons black bean sauce
- 2 teaspoons sugar
- 2 teaspoons soy sauce
- 1 teaspoon dark soy sauce

FOR THE STIR FRY:

- 2 tablespoons peanut oil
- 1-inch piece ginger, peeled and minced
- 2 garlic cloves, minced
- 1 scallion, chopped

1. Pour the Shaoxing wine, cornstarch, salt, and pepper over the pork and toss to combine. Marinate at room temperature for about 20 minutes.
2. In a small bowl, prepare the sauce by mixing together the water, black bean sauce, sugar, soy sauce, and dark soy sauce. Set it aside.
3. In a wok over medium-high heat, heat the peanut oil.
4. Arrange the pork ribs in the wok in a single layer. Let them cook without stirring for 30 seconds, add the ginger and garlic, then flip the ribs with a wok spatula.
5. Cook, stirring every 10 seconds or so, for about 2 minutes.
6. Add the sauce, stir, and cover the wok.
7. Reduce the heat to low and simmer for about 20 minutes. Peek every few minutes to make sure the sauce is not evaporating too quickly. If it is, add water when necessary to keep it simmering until the last minute.
8. Transfer the ribs to a serving plate and garnish with the chopped scallion. Serve immediately.

Honeyed Sauce with Five-Spice Pork

Prep time: 15 minutes | Cook time: ⅓ minutes | Serves 4 to 6

FOR THE MARINADE:

- 2 teaspoons Shaoxing wine
- 2 teaspoons cornstarch
- ½ teaspoon Chinese five-spice powder
- ½ teaspoon salt
- Pinch ground white pepper
- 1 pound pork tenderloin or shoulder, cut into thin strips

FOR THE SAUCE:

- 1 tablespoon soy sauce
- 2 teaspoons honey
- ½ teaspoon brown sugar
- ½ teaspoon dark soy sauce
- ½ teaspoon Chinese five-spice powder

FOR THE STIR FRY:

- 2 tablespoons peanut oil
- 2 garlic cloves, minced

1. Pour the Shaoxing wine, cornstarch, five-spice powder, salt, and pepper over the pork and toss to combine. Marinate at room temperature for 20 minutes.
2. In a small bowl, prepare the sauce by combining the soy sauce, honey, brown sugar, dark soy sauce, and five-spice powder.
3. In a wok over medium-high heat, heat the peanut oil.
4. Add the pork and Stir-fry until slightly golden brown.
5. Add the garlic and Stir-fry for about 20 seconds.
6. Stir in the sauce, tossing well to coat the pork, and transfer to a serving dish. Serve immediately.

Chili Bean Paste with Pork
Prep time: 10 minutes | Cook time: 1⅓ minutes | Serves 4

- 1 pound (454 g) pork shoulder
- Water, for boiling pork shoulder
- For the Sauce:
- 1 tablespoon black bean paste
- 1 tablespoon soy sauce
- 1 teaspoon chili bean paste
- ½ teaspoon sugar
- Pinch salt
- For the Stir Fry:
- 1 tablespoon peanut oil
- 2 garlic cloves, minced
- 1 leek, cut into 1-inch pieces
- 1 green bell pepper, cut into bite-size pieces

1. Fill a medium pot with enough water to cover the pork shoulder. Bring the water to a boil over high heat and lower the pork into the pot.
2. Reduce the heat to medium, cover, and simmer for 20 minutes.
3. Remove the pork from the water and let it cool. Keep it in the refrigerator until you are ready to cook the dish.
4. In a small bowl, prepare the sauce by mixing together the black bean paste, soy sauce, chili bean paste, sugar, and salt.
5. When the meat has cooled and you are ready to prepare the dish, slice it into the thinnest pieces possible with a very sharp knife.
6. In a wok over medium-high heat, heat the peanut oil.
7. Add the pork and Stir-fry the slices until they turn slightly brown around the edges. Remove the pork from the wok and set it aside.
8. Add more oil to the wok if needed, add the garlic, and Stir-fry for about 20 seconds, until aromatic.
9. Add the leek and bell pepper, Stir-fry for about 1 minute, and return the pork to the wok.
10. Add the black bean sauce, stir well, and transfer the dish to a serving plate.

Cumin Beef and Spinach Stir-fry
Prep time: 5 minutes | Cook time: 10 minutes| Serves 2

- 1/2 pound beef
  1 cup sliced spinach
- 1 cup sliced Chinese celery
- 1/2 cup sliced onions
- 1 Tbsp. coconut oil
- 2 Tsp. ground cumin

1. Marinade beef in a Superfoods marinade (add ground cumin).
2. Stir-frydrained beef in coconut oil for few minutes, add onions and Chinese celery and Stir-fryfor 2 more minutes.
3. Add the rest of the marinade and spinach and Stir-fryfor a minute.
4. Serve with brown rice or quinoa.

Bitter Gourd and Minced Meat Stir-fry
Prep time: 5 minutes | Cook time: 10 minutes| Serves 2

- 1/2 pound minced beef
  2 cups sliced bitter gourd
- 1/2 cup sprouts
- 1/2 cup sliced onions
- 1 Tbsp. coconut oil

1. Marinade minced beef in a Superfoods marinade.
2. Stir-frydrained minced beef in coconut oil for few minutes, add all vegetables and Stir-fryfor 2 more minutes.
3. Add the rest of the marinade and Stir-fryfor a minute.
4. Serve with brown rice or quinoa.

Beef and Snow Peas Stir-fry
Prep time: 5 minutes | Cook time: 10 minutes| Serves 2

- 1/2 pound beef
  2 cups sliced snow peas
- 1/2 of the small onion, sliced
- 1 Tbsp. coconut oil
- 1 Tsp. red pepper flakes

1. Marinade beef in a Superfoods marinade (add red pepper flakes).
2. Stir-frydrained beef in coconut oil for few minutes, add onions and Snow Peas and Stir-fryfor 2 more minutes.
3. Add the rest of the marinade and Stir-fryfor a minute.
4. Serve with brown rice or quinoa.

Beef and Yellow Peppers Stir-fry
Prep time: 5 minutes | Cook time: 10 minutes| Serves 2

- 1/2 pound beef
  2 sliced yellow peppers
- 1 sliced red or orange pepper
- 1/2 cup sliced onions
- 1 Tbsp. coconut oil
- 1/2 cup broccoli florets
- 1/2 cup mushrooms
- 1/2 cup sliced zucchini or celery or both

1. Marinade beef in a Superfoods marinade.
2. Stir-frydrained beef in coconut oil for few minutes, add all veggies and Stir-fryfor 2 more minutes.
3. Add the rest of the marinade and Stir-fryfor a minute.
4. Serve with brown rice or quinoa.

Bok Choy and Seaweed Stir-fry
Prep time: 5 minutes | Cook time: 10 minutes | Serves 2

- 2 cups sliced Bok Choy
- 1/2 cup dried mixed seaweed
- 1/2 cup julienned carrots
- 2 tbsp. bonito flakes
- 1 Tbsp. coconut oil

1. Put the dried seaweed in lots of water and soak for 10-15 minutes.
2. At the same time marinade sliced bok choy in Superfoods marinade for 15 minutes.
3. Stir-frydrained bok choy in coconut oil for 1 minute, add carrots, squeezed out seaweed and the rest of the marinade and Stir-fryfor 1 more minute.
4. Top with bonito flakes. Serve with brown rice or quinoa.

Okra, Ground Beef, Red Peppers and Cilantro Stir-fry
Prep time: 5 minutes | Cook time: 10 minutes | Serves 2

- 1/2 pound ground beef
  1 cup sliced okra
- 1 cup sliced red peppers
- 1/2 cup sliced onions
- 1/4 cup sliced cilantro
- 1 Tbsp. coconut oil

1. Marinade okra in a Superfoods marinade.
2. Stir-frydrained okra and ground beef in coconut oil for few minutes, add red peppers and onions and Stir-fryfor 2 more minutes.
3. Add the rest of the marinade and half of cilantro and Stir-fryfor a minute. Decorate with the rest of cilantro.
4. Serve with brown rice or quinoa.

Pork, Broccoli, Baby Carrots and Mushrooms Stir-fry
Prep time: 5 minutes | Cook time: 10 minutes | Serves 2

- 1/2 pound cubed pork
  1 cup sliced broccoli
- 1 cup halved lengthwise baby carrots
- 1/2 cup sliced mushrooms
- 1 Tbsp. coconut oil

1. Marinade pork in a Superfoods marinade.
2. Stir-frydrained pork in coconut oil for few minutes, add broccoli and baby carrots and Stir-fryfor 2 more minutes.
3. Add the rest of the marinade and mushrooms and Stir-fryfor a minute.
4. Serve with brown rice or quinoa.

Pork, Red Peppers, Broccoli and Carrots Stir-fry
Prep time: 5 minutes | Cook time: 10 minutes | Serves 2

- 1/2 pound pork
  1 cup sliced red peppers
- 1 cup sliced broccoli
- 1/2 cup sliced carrots
- 1 Tbsp. coconut oil

1. Marinade pork in a Superfoods marinade.
2. Stir-frydrained pork in coconut oil for few minutes, add broccoli and carrots and Stir-fryfor 2 more minutes.
3. Add the rest of the marinade and red peppers and Stir-fryfor a minute.
4. Serve with brown rice or quinoa.

Green Peas, Pork, Onions and Cilntro Stir-fry
Prep time: 5 minutes | Cook time: 10 minutes | Serves 2

- 1/2 pound pork
  1 cup green peas
- 1 cup sliced onions
- 1/4 cup cilantro
- 1 Tbsp. coconut oil

1. Marinade pork in a Superfoods marinade.
2. Stir-frydrained pork and green peas in coconut oil for few minutes, add onions and Stir-fryfor 2 more minutes.
3. Add the rest of the marinade and Stir-fryfor a minute.
4. Serve with brown rice or quinoa.

Asparagus With Lap Cheong Chinese Sausage And Peanuts
Prep time: 10 minutes | Cook time: 10 minutes | Serves 4

- 1 tablespoon toasted sesame oil
- ⅓ pound lap cheong, sliced diagonally into ¼-inch pieces (2–3 links)
- 2 cups of asparagus ends removed and diagonally cut and trimmed into 2 inch pieces
- 2 tablespoons Shaoxing wine
- ½ cup of peanuts coarsely chopped
- 2 tablespoons oyster sauce

1. Heat the sesame oil and lap cheong over high heat until sausage is lightly browned, about 2 minutes.
2. Add the asparagus and Stir-fryfor 1 minute.
3. Add in the wine and Stir-fryfor 1 minute.
4. Add the peanuts and Stir-fryfor 1 minute.
5. Add the oyster sauce and toss just before serving over rice or noodles.

Chapter 8
Seafood

Shrimp with Lobster Sauce

Prep time: 5 minutes | Cook time: 5 minutes | Serves 4 to 6

FOR THE SAUCE

- 1 cup chicken broth
- 2 teaspoons light soy sauce
- 2 teaspoons cornstarch
- 1 teaspoon Shaoxing cooking wine
- ½ teaspoon sugar
- Pinch ground white pepper
- For the Stir Fry
- 1 tablespoon cooking oil
- 2-inch piece ginger, julienned
- 2 garlic cloves, minced
- ½ cup frozen peas and carrots
- 1 pound large shrimp, peeled and deveined
- 1 large egg, lightly beaten

TO MAKE THE SAUCE

1. In a small bowl, combine the chicken broth, soy sauce, cornstarch, wine, sugar, and white pepper. Stir well, breaking up any lumps. Set aside.
2. To make the Stir Fry
3. In the wok, heat the oil over medium-high heat until it shimmers.
4. Add the ginger and garlic and Stir-fryuntil aromatic, or for about 20 seconds.
5. Add the frozen peas and carrots and Stir-fryfor 10 seconds to mix.
6. Pour in the sauce and the shrimp. Stir with a wok spatula to combine all the ingredients.
7. Slowly pour in the beaten egg while using the wok spatula to swirl it into the sauce.
8. As soon as the shrimp are cooked—when they curl into a "C" shape—transfer the dish to a serving plate and serve immediately.

Drunken Shrimp

Prep time: 30 minutes | Cook time: 10 minutes | Serves 4

- 2 cups Shaoxing cooking wine
- 4 peeled fresh ginger slices, each about the size of a quarter
- 2 tablespoons dried goji berries (optional)
- 2 teaspoons sugar
- 1 pound jumbo shrimp, peeled and deveined, tails left on
- 2 tablespoons cooking oil
- Kosher salt
- 2 teaspoons cornstarch

1. In a wide mixing bowl, stir together the wine, ginger, goji berries (if using), and sugar until the sugar is dissolved. Add the shrimp and cover. Marinate in the refrigerator for 20 to 30 minutes.
2. Pour the shrimp and marinade into a colander set over a bowl. Reserve ½ cup of the marinade and discard the rest.
3. In the wok, heat the oil over medium-high heat

until it shimmers. Season the oil by adding a small pinch of salt, and swirl gently.

4. Add the shrimp and vigorously Stir Fry, adding a pinch of salt as you flip and toss the shrimp around in the wok. Keep moving the shrimp around for about 3 minutes, until they just turn pink.
5. Stir the cornstarch into the reserved marinade and pour it over the shrimp. Toss the shrimp and coat with the marinade. It will thicken into a glossy sauce as it begins to boil, about another 5 minutes more.
6. Transfer the shrimp and goji berries to a platter, discard the ginger, and serve hot.

Kung Pao Shrimp

Prep time: 5 minutes | Cook time: 10 minutes | Serves 4 to 6

FOR THE SAUCE

- 2 tablespoons rice vinegar
- 2 tablespoons light soy sauce
- 2 teaspoons brown sugar
- 1 teaspoon dark soy sauce
- 1 teaspoon sesame oil
- 1 teaspoon cornstarch
- For the Stir Fry
- 2 tablespoons cooking oil
- 8 to 10 dried red chiles
- 1 small green bell pepper (or ½ a large one), cut into bite-size pieces
- 2-inch piece ginger, julienned
- 2 garlic cloves, crushed and chopped
- 1 pound shrimp, peeled and deveined
- ¼ cup unsalted roasted peanuts
- 1 or 2 scallions, both white and green parts, cut into 1-inch pieces
- Steamed rice, for serving

TO MAKE THE SAUCE

1. In a small bowl, combine the rice vinegar, light soy sauce, brown sugar, dark soy sauce, sesame oil, and cornstarch. Mix well and set aside.

TO MAKE THE STIR FRY

2. In the wok, heat the cooking oil over medium heat until it shimmers.
3. Add the chiles and bell pepper and Stir-fryfor 3 minutes, allowing the skin of the bell pepper to blister.
4. Add the ginger and garlic and Stir-fryuntil aromatic, about 20 seconds.
5. Add the shrimp, spreading them in a single layer. Cook the bottom side of the shrimp, then flip and Stir-fry them for about 1 minute, or until fully cooked.
6. Add the roasted peanuts and stir in the sauce.
7. When the sauce thickens, turn off the heat and toss in the scallions. Transfer to a serving dish and serve with steamed rice.

Whole Steamed Fish with Sizzling Ginger and Scallions (Hong Zheng Yu)

Prep time: 10 minutes |Cook time: 20 minutes |Serves 4

FOR THE FISH

- 1 whole whitefish, about 2 pounds, head on and cleaned
- ½ cup kosher salt, for cleaning
- 3 scallions, both white and green parts, sliced into 3-inch pieces
- 4 peeled, fresh ginger slices, each about the size of a quarter
- 2 tablespoons Shaoxing cooking wine
- For the sauce
- 2 tablespoons light soy sauce
- 1 tablespoon sesame oil
- 2 teaspoons sugar
- For the sizzling ginger oil
- 3 tablespoons cooking oil
- 2 tablespoons peeled fresh ginger, finely julienned into thin strips, divided
- 2 scallions, both white and green parts, thinly sliced, divided
- Red onion, thinly sliced (optional)
- Chopped fresh cilantro (optional)

TO MAKE THE FISH

1. Rub the fish inside and out with the kosher salt. Rinse the fish and pat dry with paper towels.
2. On a plate large enough to fit into a bamboo steamer basket, make a bed using half of each of the scallions and ginger. Lay the fish on top and stuff the remaining scallions and ginger inside the fish. Pour the wine over the fish.
3. Rinse a bamboo steamer basket and its lid under cold water and place it in the wok. Pour in about 2 inches of cold water, or until it is above the bottom rim of the steamer by about ¼ to ½ inch, but not so high that the water touches the bottom of the basket. Bring the water to a boil.
4. Place the plate in the steamer basket and cover. Steam the fish over medium heat for 15 minutes (add 2 minutes for every half pound more). Before removing from the wok, poke the fish with a fork near the head. If the flesh flakes, it's done. If the flesh still sticks together, steam for 2 minutes more.
5. While the fish is steaming, in a small pan, warm the soy sauce, sesame oil, and sugar over low heat. Set aside.
6. Once the fish is cooked, transfer to a clean platter. Discard the cooking liquid and aromatics from the steaming plate. Pour the warm soy sauce mixture over the fish. Tent with foil to keep it warm while you prepare the oil.

TO MAKE THE SIZZLING GINGER OIL

7. In a small saucepan, heat the cooking oil over medium heat. Just before it starts to smoke, add half of each of the ginger and scallions and fry for 10 seconds. Pour the hot, sizzling oil over the top of the fish.
8. Garnish with the remaining ginger, scallions, red onion (if using), and cilantro (if using) and serve immediately.

Steamed Ginger, Garlic, and Scallion Salmon

Prep time: 10 minutes |Cook time: 10 minutes |Serves 4

- 1½ pounds fresh salmon fillet
- 2 tablespoons chopped fresh ginger
- 4 garlic cloves, crushed and chopped
- 4 scallions, both white and green parts, minced
- ¼ cup dark soy sauce
- Rice, for serving

1. Cut the salmon fillet into 4 pieces and put in a pie pan or shallow dish for steaming.
2. Lightly score the fillets about halfway through with perpendicular cuts 1 inch apart.
3. In a small bowl, mix the ginger, garlic, scallions, soy sauce, and wine together to form a coarse pesto.
4. Spread the pesto on top of the fillet, being sure to press it into the cuts.
5. In the wok, bring 1 inch of water to a boil over high heat. Place a rack in the wok and the pan on the rack. Cover and steam the fish for 5 minutes per inch of thickness for medium rare. It will be opaque and flaky when poked with a fork or chopstick.
6. Serve over rice.

Smoked-Tea Tilapia

Prep time: 10 minutes |Cook time: 15 minutes |Serves 4

- 1 pound fresh tilapia fillets (3 or 4 fillets)
- 2 tablespoons Shaoxing cooking wine
- 2 tablespoons light soy sauce
- 1 tablespoon toasted sesame oil
- ¼ cup uncooked long-grain white rice
- ¼ cup loose black oolong tea
- 2 tablespoons brown sugar
- Rice, for serving
- Vegetables, for serving

1. In a zip-top bag, combine the tilapia, wine, soy sauce, and sesame oil and massage to cover it on all sides.
2. Combine the rice, tea leaves, and brown sugar on a square piece of aluminum foil and roll the edges up to form the foil into a shallow, ½-inch-deep saucer. The top should be open. Place the foil saucer in the bottom of the wok.
3. Place a rack in the wok and put the fish on the rack above the mixture. Cover with a domed lid.
4. If you're cooking indoors, open any windows near the stove and turn your exhaust fan on high. If you don't have a way to exhaust air outside, do the next steps outdoors.
5. Turn the heat on high. As the mixture heats, it will begin to smoke. First the smoke will be white, then light yellow, then darker yellow. When it turns dark yellow (about 5 minutes), turn the heat to low.
6. Allow the fish to smoke on low for 5 minutes, then turn the heat off and wait 5 minutes before checking the fish. It will be dark golden brown and flaky.
7. Serve over rice with a side of vegetables.

Honey Walnut Shrimp
Prep time: 10 minutes | Cook time: 10 minutes | Serves 2 to 4

- 1 cup water
- 1 cup sugar
- 1 cup walnuts
- 1 large egg
- ¼ cup cornstarch
- 1 teaspoon kosher salt
- ½ teaspoon ground white pepper
- 1 pound medium shrimp, peeled and deveined
- ¼ cup vegetable oil
- 2 tablespoons crushed and chopped fresh ginger
- 3 garlic cloves, crushed and chopped
- 1 medium onion, diced into ½-inch pieces
- 1 red bell pepper, diced into ½-inch pieces
- 1 bunch (6 to 8) scallions, cut into ½-inch pieces
- ¼ cup honey
- ¼ cup mayonnaise
- 2 tablespoons rice wine
- 2 tablespoons soy sauce
- Steamed rice, for serving
- Chopped cilantro, for serving (optional)

1. In a small pan, heat the water and sugar over medium-high heat until the water boils and the sugar dissolves.
2. Add the walnuts and boil for 1 minute. Transfer the walnuts to paper towels to drain.
3. Beat the egg in a small bowl. In another small bowl, combine the cornstarch, salt, and white pepper.
4. Dip the shrimp in the egg, one at a time, to coat, then dredge in the cornstarch mixture, coating evenly.
5. In the wok or a large cast-iron skillet, heat the oil over high heat until it shimmers. Add the coated shrimp and Stir-fryfor about 3 minutes, until golden brown. Transfer the fried shrimp to a plate.
6. Remove and discard all but 2 tablespoons of oil from the pan. Add the ginger and garlic and Stir-fryfor about 1 minute, until lightly browned.
7. Add the onion and Stir-fryfor 1 minute. Add the bell pepper and Stir-fryfor 1 minute. Add the scallions and Stir-fryfor 1 minute.
8. In a medium bowl, whisk together the honey, mayonnaise, rice wine, and soy sauce. Pour the sauce into the wok and cook, stirring, for about 2 minutes, until a glaze forms. Add the walnuts and shrimp, tossing to coat.
9. Serve over steamed rice. Optionally, garnish with cilantro.

Shrimp and Squid Stir-fry with Bok Choy
Prep time: 10 minutes | Cook time: 5 minutes | Serves 4

- 8 ounces large shrimp, shelled, deveined, and cut in half lengthwise
- 8 ounces squid tentacles and/or rings
- 4 tablespoons Shaoxing cooking wine, divided
- 4 tablespoons light soy sauce, divided
- 2 tablespoons toasted sesame oil, divided
- 2 tablespoons cornstarch, divided
- 2 tablespoons cooking oil
- 1 tablespoon chopped fresh ginger
- 2 garlic cloves, crushed and chopped
- 1 (15-ounce) can straw mushrooms, drained and rinsed
- 2 cups bok choy cut into ½-inch pieces
- 4 scallions, both white and green parts, cut into ¼-inch pieces
- Rice or noodles, for serving

1. In two medium bowls, velvet the shrimp and squid separately by combining half the wine, soy sauce, sesame oil, and cornstarch in each bowl.
2. In the wok, heat the cooking oil over medium-high heat until it shimmers.
3. Add the ginger, garlic, and shrimp, reserving any liquid, and Stir-fryfor 2 minutes, until fragrant.
4. Add the mushrooms and Stir-fryfor 1 minute, until the shrimp is opaque.
5. Add the bok choy and Stir-fryfor 1 minute, until bright green.
6. Add the squid and Stir-fryfor 1 minute, reserving any liquid, until the squid curls.
7. Add the remaining liquids and scallions and Stir-fryfor 1 minute to form a light glaze. Serve over rice or noodles.

Steamed Shrimp and Scallops with Straw Mushrooms in Oyster Sauce
Prep time: 10 minutes | Cook time: 10 minutes | Serves 4

- 8 ounces large shrimp, shelled, deveined, and cut in half lengthwise
- 8 ounces fresh sea scallops. sliced in half coin-wise
- 1 (15-ounce) can straw mushrooms, drained and rinsed
- ¼ cup oyster sauce
- 4 ounces ground pork
- 4 scallions, both white and green parts, cut into ¼-inch pieces
- Rice or noodles, for serving

1. In a pie pan or shallow dish, combine the sliced shrimp, scallops, and mushrooms.
2. Mix the oyster sauce and ground pork with chopsticks so it is loosely clumped, then sprinkle the pork evenly over the ingredients in the pie pan.
3. Sprinkle the scallions over everything.
4. In the wok, bring 1 inch of water to a boil over high heat. Place a rack in the wok and the pie pan on the rack. Cover and steam for 10 minutes, or until cooked through.
5. Serve over rice or noodles.

Sichuan Boiled Codfish (Shui Zhu Yu)
Prep time: 10 minutes |Cook time: 10 minutes |Serves 4

1 pound codfish fillet, cut into ½-inch strips
2 tablespoons Shaoxing cooking wine
2 tablespoons light soy sauce
1 tablespoon cornstarch
¼ cup cooking oil
1 tablespoon chopped fresh ginger
4 garlic cloves, crushed and chopped
1 teaspoon Chinese five spice powder
1 teaspoon dried Sichuan peppercorns
1 tablespoon spicy sesame oil
4 cups chicken broth
½ ounce dried, sliced, shiitake mushrooms
1 cup napa cabbage cut into 1-inch strips
4 scallions, both white and green parts, cut into ¼-inch pieces

1. In a shallow dish, combine the sliced fish, wine, soy sauce, and cornstarch.
2. In the wok, heat the oil over medium-high heat until it shimmers.
3. Add the ginger, garlic, five-spice powder, Sichuan peppercorns, and spicy sesame oil and Stir-fryfor 1 minute, until fragrant.
4. Add the chicken broth and mushrooms and bring to a boil for 5 minutes, until the mushrooms are tender.
5. Add the sliced fish, napa cabbage, and scallions to the broth and simmer for 2 minutes, until the fish is opaque. Serve immediately in warmed bowls.

Shrimp, Corn and Leeks Stir Fry
Prep time: 5 minutes | Cook time: 10 minutes| Serves 2

- 1 sliced carrot
  1/2 pound shrimp
- 1 cup drained corn
- 1 cup sliced onions
- 1 Tbsp. oil

1. Marinade shrimp in Superfoods marinade.
2. Stir-frydrained shrimp in coconut oil for few minutes, add all vegetables and Stir-fryfor 2 more minutes.
3. Add the rest of the marinade and Stir-fryfor a minute. Serve with brown rice or quinoa.

Mixed Seafood, Snow Peas and Celery Stir Fry
Prep time: 5 minutes | Cook time: 10 minutes| Serves 2

- 1 sliced carrot
  1/2 pound mixed seafood
- 1 cup sliced snow peas
- 1 cup sliced celery
- 1/2 cup sliced onions
- 1 Tbsp. oil

1. Marinade mixed seafood in Superfoods marinade.
2. Stir-frydrained mixed seafood in coconut oil for few minutes, add all vegetables and Stir-fryfor 2 more minutes.
3. Add the rest of the marinade and Stir-fryfor a minute. Serve with brown rice or quinoa.

Shrimp, Carrot, Red Peppers and Green Onion Stir Fry
Prep time: 5 minutes | Cook time: 10 minutes| Serves 2

- 1/2-pound shrimp
  1 cup red peppers
- 1/2 cup sliced carrots
- 1/2 cup sliced green onions
- 1 Tbsp. coconut oil

1. Marinade shrimp in a Superfoods marinade.
2. Stir-frydrained shrimp in coconut oil for few minutes, add all vegetables and Stir-fryfor 2 more minutes.
3. Add the rest of the marinade and Stir-fryfor a minute.
4. Serve with brown rice or quinoa.

Fish, Sprouts, Chinese Celery and Dill Stir Fry
Prep time: 5 minutes | Cook time: 10 minutes| Serves 2

- 1/2 pound fish of your choice
  2 cups sprouts
- 2 cup sliced Chinese celery
- 1/2 cup sliced dill
- 1 Tbsp. coconut oil

1. Marinade fish in a Superfoods marinade.
2. Stir-frydrained fish in coconut oil for few minutes, add all vegetables and Stir-fryfor 2 more minutes.
3. Add the rest of the marinade and Stir-fryfor a minute.
4. Serve with brown rice or quinoa.

Fish, Wood Ear Mushrooms and Green Peas Stir Fry

Prep time: 5 minutes | Cook time: 10 minutes| Serves 2

- 1/2 pound fish filets (e.g. tilapia, cod, sole, flounder) 1 cup wood ear mushrooms, soaked in water for 30 minutes
- 1/2 cup green peas
- 1 Tbsp. coconut oil

1. Marinade fish in a Superfoods marinade.
2. Stir-frydrained fish and green peas in coconut oil for 4-5 more minutes.
3. Add the rest of the marinade, mushrooms and Stir-fryfor a minute.
4. Serve with brown rice or quinoa.

Asian Style Fried Rice with Prawns and Pineapple

Prep time: 15 minutes |Cook time: 50 minutes | Serves 4

- 1.8 kg pineapple
- 1/2 cup paprika
- 3 thinly sliced spring onions
- 2 teaspoons of chopped fresh jalapeño pepper
- 1/2 tablespoon of soy sauce
- 1/2 teaspoon of sugar
- 1 teaspoon of anchovy paste
- 1/2 teaspoon turmeric
- 2 tablespoons of vegetable oil
- 1 pound small shrimp (about 50(peeled and chopped
- 2 cloves of chopped garlic
- 5 cups of cooked rice

1. Cut the pineapple in half lengthways, cut out the pulp, leaving 1.2 cm thick pods and reserve the peel. Discard the core and cut enough of the pineapple into pieces to measure 1 1/2 peels and reserve the remaining pineapple for other use.
2. Mix the pineapple pieces, paprika, spring onions and jalapeño pepper in a bowl. In a small bowl, stir together the soy sauce, sugar, anchovy paste, turmeric and 1 tablespoon of water. Heat 1 tablespoon of oil in a wok or heavy pan over moderate heat until hot but not smoked, fry the prawns in it for 1 1/2 minutes or until just firm, stirring, and transfer to a bowl.
3. Heat the remaining 1 tablespoon of oil over moderate heat until it is hot but not smoking, and fry the garlic in the oil for 5 seconds while stirring or until it is golden brown. Add the rice and saute the mixture for 30 seconds or until the rice is hot. Add the soy mixture and sauté the mixture for 1 minute while stirring.
4. Add the pineapple mixture and prawns, sauté the mixture for 1 minute or until hot, then stir in the coriander. Serve the fried rice in the reserved pineapple bowls as desired. (Fried rice is served separately).

Spicy Hunan-Style Fish

Prep time: 10 minutes | Cook time: 10 minutes | Serves 2

- 1½ pounds (680 g) fresh tilapia
- 16 ounces (454 g) silken tofu
- ⅛ teaspoon salt
- 3 tablespoons canola oil
- 1 ½ tablespoons ginger, minced
- 6 tablespoons duo jiao
- 3 garlic cloves, minced
- 1 scallion, diced
- ⅔ cup hot water
- 2 tablespoons soy sauce
- 1 teaspoon sugar
- ¼ teaspoon white pepper

1. Mix hot water, soy sauce, sugar, white pepper, garlic, ginger, salt, scallions, and Duo Jiao in a Mandarin wok.
2. Cook this sauce until the sauce is reduced to half, then allow it to cool.
3. Soak the tofu and fillets in the prepared sauce, rub well, and cover to marinate for 30 minutes.
4. Add oil to a cooking pan and place it over medium heat.
5. Sear the tofu and fish in the skillet for 5 minutes per side until golden-brown.
6. Serve warm.

Spiced Shrimp with Garlic

Prep time: 10 minutes | Cook time: 7 minutes | Serves 6

- 1 pound (454 g) large, head-on shrimp
- ¼ teaspoon white pepper powder
- 2 teaspoons Shaoxing wine
- 3 to 4 ginger slices, minced
- 7 garlic cloves, minced
- 2 scallions, chopped
- 3 red chilies, chopped
- 1 cup panko breadcrumbs
- 1 cup vegetable oil
- ½ teaspoon salt
- ¼ teaspoon sugar
- ⅛ teaspoon five-spice powder

1. Sauté ginger and garlic with vegetable oil in a Mandarin wok until golden-brown.
2. Stir in white pepper, wine, red chilies, scallions, salt, sugar, and spice powder.
3. Mix and toss in shrimp, then cook for 5 to 6 minutes.
4. Spread the shrimp in a baking dish and drizzle the panko crumbs on top.
5. Bake the shrimp for 2 minutes in the oven at 350°F (180°C).
6. Serve warm.

Sauce with Shrimp and Broccoli
Prep time: 10 minutes | Cook time: 5 minutes | Serves 8

- 16 shrimps, peeled, deveined, and butterflied
- 10 ounces (283 g) broccoli florets
- ½ cup chicken stock
- ¼ teaspoon granulated sugar
- 1½ tablespoons soy sauce
- ½ teaspoon dark soy sauce
- 1 tablespoon oyster sauce
- ½ teaspoon sesame oil
- ⅛ teaspoon white pepper
- 2 tablespoons canola oil
- 2 garlic cloves, chopped
- 1 tablespoon Shaoxing wine
- 1½ tablespoons cornstarch, whisked with 2 tablespoons water

1. Add sesame oil to a large wok and stir in garlic.
2. Sauté until the garlic turns golden, then add broccoli.
3. Stir and cook for 5 minutes until soft.
4. Add shrimp, sugar, soy sauce, chicken stock, oyster sauce, white pepper, and wine to the saucepan.
5. Cook the mixture until the shrimp are tender.
6. Stir in cornstarch, mix and cook until the mixture thickens.
7. Serve warm.

Eggy Shrimp Tempura
Prep time: 10 minutes | Cook time: 1½ minutes | Serves 4

- 1 cup all-purpose flour
- 2 tablespoons cornstarch
- 1 pinch salt
- 1 cup water
- 1 egg yolk
- 2 egg whites, lightly beaten
- 450 g Medium-sized shrimp, peeled and peeled
- 2 cups vegetable oil for frying

1. Heat the oil in a deep fryer to 190°F (88°C) and whisk the flour, cornstarch and salt in a large bowl. Make a well in the middle of the flour.
2. Mix in the water and egg yolk. Mix only until it is damp; the dough becomes lumpy. Stir in the egg whites and dip the prawns one after the other in the batter.
3. Carefully place a few prawns one after the other in the hot oil. Fry for 1½ minutes until golden brown. Drain on paper towels.

Milky Fish Masala
Prep time: 15 minutes | Cook time: 8⅓ minutes | Serves 4 to 6

- 1 can unsweetened coconut milk, not shaken
- 2 tablespoons coconut oil or rapeseed oil
- 2 teaspoons black mustard seeds
- 5 slices of peeled crushed fresh ginger
- 2 large cloves of crushed garlic
- 1 to 4 fresh hot green chilies such as Thai or Serrano, halved lengthways
- 2 tablespoons ground coriander
- ½ teaspoon ground turmeric
- ½ teaspoon curry powder
- 3 medium-sized tomatoes, roughly chopped
- ¾ cup water
- 900 g black sea bass fillet including skin, cut into cubes
- ¾ teaspoon salt
- ⅓ cup diced mango
- Boiled rice

1. Take a scoop of ¼ cup heavy cream from the top of the coconut milk from the can. Set aside the milk and remaining cream for another use.
2. Heat a wok with oil over medium heat until the pan is hot but not smoking. Add the mustard seeds and cook for 15 seconds or until the seeds make a popping sound. Stir in the chilies, ginger and garlic and stir for 1 minute.
3. Stir in the chili powder, curry powder, coriander and turmeric for 5 to 10 seconds until it is fragrant. Stir in the tomatoes and cook for 1 minute. Stir in water and bring to a boil.
4. Reduce the heat setting, cover the pan and let it simmer for 5 minutes. Add the coconut cream and stir until well mixed. Then add the fish and the salt and simmer without the lid for 3 to 5 minutes or until the fish is just cooked through, stirring occasionally.
5. Carefully add the mango and stir in.
6. Serve it with rice.

Avocado with Crab and Corn Salad

Prep time: 10 minutes | Cook time: 4 minutes | Serve 6

- 4 ears of corn, kernels cut from the cob
- 2 leeks, only the white parts, thinly sliced
- 2 garlic cloves, chopped
- 2 avocados, peeled, pitted and diced into pieces
- ½ lemon, squeezed
- 5 tablespoons vegetable oil
- 1 tablespoon rice vinegar
- 1 tablespoon vegetable oil
- 1 tablespoon rice vinegar
- 1 tablespoon fresh basil, chopped
- 1 teaspoon salt
- ½ teaspoon chopped fresh tarragon
- 2 cans lumpy crab meat, drained and flaked

1. Put the corn kernels in a sieve to separate the small pieces; put in a bowl. In a separate bowl, stir together the lemon juice and diced avocado so they don't turn brown.
2. Heat vegetable oil in a pan over high heat; Add corn mixture. Cook for 4 to 8 minutes, stirring, until the corn is evenly brown.
3. Mix the tarragon, corn mixture, salt, avocado, basil and rice vinegar in a serving bowl.
4. Put the crab meat on top.

Prawns with Shiitake Mushrooms and Baby Bok Choy

Prep time: 15 minutes | Cook time: 50 minutes | Serves 4

- 1 1/2 cups of chicken broth
- 5 tablespoons of fish sauce and 1 tablespoon of granulated sugar
- 12 plantation or tiger prawns
- 110 g shiitake mushrooms
- 400 to 450 g Baby-Bok Choy
- 3 tablespoons of rapeseed oil
- 1/2 teaspoon of minced garlic
- 2 tablespoons mirin (rice wine)
- 1/3 cup Stir-frysauce
- Steamed rice for serving

FOR THE STIR-FRYSAUCE:

Mix the fish sauce, sugar, and chicken broth in a medium bowl. Mix well until the sugar has completely dissolved.

FOR THE PRAWNS:

1. 1.Peel the shells of the shrimp and cut the shrimp in half lengthways. Core the shrimp. Rinse the shrimp under cold water, pat dry with paper towels, and set aside. Clean the shiitake mushrooms with a brush or a dry, clean towel.
2. 2.Cut the mushrooms into pieces. Rinse the baby bok choi and cut it into pieces. Set aside and let dry. Heat a skillet or wok over high heat until the pan smokes. Add 1 tablespoon of oil to the pan.

Add the shrimp and cook for 20-30 seconds until the shrimp change color.

3. Remove the prawns from the pan and set aside. Without cleaning the pan, add the remaining 2 tablespoons of oil. Add the garlic and sauté for about 10 seconds until fragrant. Add the bok choy and mushrooms. Fry for 30 seconds to 1 minute, stirring, until vegetables are soft. Add the prawns to the vegetable mixture and Stir-fryfor 10 seconds.
4. Pour in the rice wine and keep stirring. Stir in the Stir-frysauce and cook for about 15 seconds, until the prawns are cooked through and well coated with the sauce. Remove the pan from the heat and serve immediately with steamed rice. The remaining sauce can be stored in the refrigerator or frozen for up to 4 days.

Sauteed Prawns with Coconut and Mustard

Prep time: 30 minutes | Cook time: 20 minutes | Serves 4

- 1 small coconut or 1 cup of thawed frozen desiccated coconut
- 2 tablespoons of brown mustard seeds
- 7 small fresh Thai chilies
- 3 tablespoons. water
- 450 g large shrimp in the shell, peeled with the tail and the first segment of the shell intact, and deveined
- 1 teaspoon of ground turmeric
- 1 teaspoon of salt
- 3 tablespoons of vegetable oil

1. Preheat the oven to 200 ° C and slide the oven rack to the middle position - pierce the 2 softest eyes of the coconut with a metal skewer, if you are using a whole coconut, drain the coconut water and discard it.
2. Put the whole coconut in the oven and bake for 15 minutes. Use a hammer to crack the shell of the coconut then remove the coconut flesh by gently prying it out with a strong knife.
3. Use the wide holes of a box grater to finely chop 1 cup of coconut meat. Use a grinder to finely grind the mustard seeds with a little salt.
4. Finely chop the whole chili pepper (without a slitand crush it together with the ground mustard seeds and a pinch of salt in a mortar and pestle until the chili pepper is finely ground.
5. Add 1 tablespoon of water. Mix everything into a paste. (Alternatively, you can chop the chili pepper very finely and mix it with the mustard seeds and water to make a paste.
6. Season the prawns with salt and turmeric.

Goong Tod Kratiem Prik Thai

Prep time: 5 minutes |Cook time: 10 minutes | Serves 4

- 8 cloves of garlic, minced or more to taste
- 2 tablespoons of tapioca flour
- 2 tablespoons of fish sauce
- 2 tablespoons of light soy sauce
- 1 tablespoon of white sugar
- 1/2 teaspoon of ground white pepper
- 1/4 cup vegetable oil, split or as needed
- 450 g unpeeled prawns, divided

1. Mix white pepper, garlic, sugar, tapioca flour, soy sauce and fish sauce in a bowl; turn the prawns in it to coat them.
2. Put half of the prawns in a single layer; Fry 1-2 minutes per side until crispy and golden brown.
3. Repeat the process with the remaining prawns and the oil.

Ginger Garlic Shrimp

Prep time: 15 minutes |Cook time: 45 minutes | Serves 4

- 450 gr. Uncooked prawns (peeled and boned
- 1 tablespoon of oriental sesame oil or vegetable oil
- 1 tablespoon of chopped garlic
- 1 tablespoon of chopped fresh ginger
- 1/4 teaspoon dried and crushed red pepper
- 3 tablespoons of soy sauce
- 2 teaspoons of cornstarch
- 1/2 cup low-salt canned chicken stock
- 1/4 cup rice vinegar
- 2 tablespoons of sugar
- 6 green onions, cut into pieces
- 1 cup of peas
- Cooked rice

1. Combine the first 5 ingredients in a medium bowl. Add 1 tablespoon of soy sauce and toss to coat. Let the soy sauce stand for 15 minutes and place the cornstarch in a small bowl.
2. Gradually add the broth and stir until the cornstarch dissolves. Mix in the vinegar, sugar and 2 tablespoons of soy sauce and heat the wok or heavy large pan over high heat.
3. Add the shrimp mixture, green onions and snow peas and Stir-fryuntil the shrimp are pink and almost cooked, about 3 minutes. Add corn starch mixture; stir until the sauce is thick, about 1 minute.
4. Serve with rice.

Fish Masala

Prep time: 30 minutes |Cook time: 10 minutes | Serves 4 - 6

- 1 can of unsweetened coconut milk (not shaken
- 2 tablespoons of coconut oil or rapeseed oil
- 2 teaspoons of black mustard seeds
- 5 slices of peeled crushed fresh ginger
- 2 large cloves of crushed garlic
- 1 to 4 fresh hot green chilies such as Thai or Serrano, halved lengthways
- 2 tablespoons of ground coriander
- 1/2 teaspoon of ground turmeric
- 1/2 teaspoon of curry powder
- 225 g tomatoes (3 medium-sized), roughly chopped (approx. 1 2/3 cups
- 3/4 cup of water
- 900 g black sea bass fillet including skin, cut into cubes
- 3/4 teaspoon salt
- 1/3 cup diced mango
- Side dish: boiled rice

1. Take a scoop of 1/4 cup of heavy cream from the top of the coconut milk from the can. Set aside the milk and remaining cream for another use.
2. Heat a wok with oil over medium heat until the pan is hot but not smoking. Add the mustard seeds and cook for 15 seconds or until the seeds make a popping sound. Stir in the chilies, ginger and garlic and stir for 1 minute.
3. Stir in the chili powder, curry powder, coriander and turmeric for 5-10 seconds until it is fragrant. Stir in the tomatoes and cook for 1 minute. Stir in water and bring to a boil.
4. Reduce the heat setting, cover the pan and let it simmer for 5 minutes. Add the coconut cream and stir until well mixed. Then add the fish and the salt and simmer without the lid for 3-5 minutes or until the fish is just cooked through, stirring occasionally.
5. Carefully add the mango and stir in.

Squid, Green Peppers and Red Peppers Stir Fry

Prep time: 5 minutes | Cook time: 10 minutes| Serves 2

- 1 cup sliced green peppers
  1/2 pound squid
- 1 cup sliced red peppers
- 1/2 cup sliced onions
- 1 Tbsp. coconut oil

1. Marinade squid in Superfoods marinade.
2. Stir-frydrained squid in coconut oil for few minutes, add all vegetables and Stir-fryfor 2 more minutes.
3. Add the rest of the marinade and Stir-fryfor a minute. Serve with brown rice or quinoa.

Crunchy Prawn Tempura
Prep time: 20 minutes |Cook time: 15 minutes | Serves 6

- 1 cup all-purpose flour
- 2 tablespoons of cornstarch
- 1 pinch of salt
- 1 cup of water
- 1 egg yolk
- 2 egg whites (lightly beaten)
- 450 g medium-sized prawns, peeled and deveined, tails left on
- 2 cups of vegetable oil for deep frying

1. Heat the oil in a deep fryer to 190 ° C.
2. In a large bowl, mix the salt, flour and cornstarch. Make a well in the center of the flour mixture. Add the egg yolks and water. Mix until the batter is almost moist and lumpy.
3. Dip the prawns one at a time in the batter and brush with it. Leave the tails uncoated with batter.
4. Carefully put the prawns piece by piece into the hot oil.
5. Fry for about 1 1/2 minutes until the topping is golden brown. Put the cooked shrimp. Tempuras on paper towels to drain off excess oil.

Chinese Take-Out Prawns
Prep time: 15 minutes |Cook time: 10 minutes | Serves 4

- 2 tablespoons of rapeseed oil
- 10 cloves of garlic (chopped)
- 1 teaspoon of chopped fresh ginger root
- 1 can of chopped water chestnuts (drained
- 1 cup of sugar peas
- 1 cup of small white mushrooms
- 1 teaspoon of crushed red pepper flakes
- 1/2 teaspoon of ground black pepper and salt
- 450 g peeled and deveined jumbo prawns
- 1/2 cup of chicken broth
- 1 tablespoon rice vinegar
- 2 tablespoons of fish sauce
- 2 tablespoons of dry sherry
- 1 tablespoon cornstarch
- 1 tablespoon of water

1. Heat a large pan or wok with oil until the oil is very hot. Add the ginger and garlic and fry in the hot oil for 30 seconds or until fragrant.
2. Mix in the mushrooms, shrimp, red pepper flakes, water chestnuts, sugar snap peas, pepper and salt. Boil and stir the mixture for 2-3 minutes until the shrimp are pink in color.
3. In a small bowl, mix rice vinegar, dry sherry, chicken broth and fish sauce together.
4. Add the sauce mixture to the shrimp mixture and cook and stir for a few seconds to mix well.
5. Mix the water and cornstarch together and add it to the wok. Cook and stir the mixture for 2 minutes or until the sauce is thick.

Chapter 9
Vegetables

Stir-Fried Chinese Cabbage with Red Chile

Prep time: 10 minutes |Cook time: 5 minutes |Serves 4

- 1 tablespoon cooking oil
- 3 garlic cloves, crushed and chopped
- 1 fresh red chile, such as red serrano, thinly sliced
- 1 pound napa cabbage, cut into 2-inch pieces
- 2 tablespoons chicken broth or water
- Sea salt

1. In the wok, heat the oil over medium-high heat until it shimmers. Stir-fry the garlic and chile for about 15 seconds, until fragrant.
2. Add the cabbage and Stir-fry for 3 minutes, until lightly browned. Add the broth and continue to Stir-fry for 2 or 3 minutes, until the cabbage is tender but not soggy.
3. Season with salt and serve.

Dry-Fried Green Beans

Prep time: 10 minutes |Cook time: 15 minutes |Serves 4

- 1 tablespoon light soy sauce
- 1 tablespoon minced garlic
- 1 tablespoon doubanjiang (Chinese chili bean paste)
- 2 teaspoons sugar
- 1 teaspoon sesame oil
- Kosher salt
- ½ cup cooking oil
- 1 pound green beans, trimmed, cut in half, and blotted dry

1. In a small bowl, stir together the soy sauce, garlic, doubanjiang, sugar, sesame oil, and a pinch of salt. Set aside.
2. In the wok, heat the cooking oil over medium-high heat to 375°F, or until it bubbles and sizzles around the end of a wooden spoon. Fry the beans in batches of a couple handfuls at a time (the beans should just cover the oil in a single layer). Gently turn the beans in the oil until they appear wrinkled, 45 seconds or 1 minute, then transfer the green beans to a paper towel–lined plate to drain.
3. Once all the beans have been cooked, carefully transfer the remaining oil to a heatproof container. Use a pair of tongs with a couple of paper towels to wipe and clean out the wok.
4. Return the wok to high heat and add 1 tablespoon of the reserved frying oil. Add the green beans and chili sauce mixture, Stir Frying until the sauce comes to a boil and coats the green beans. Transfer the beans to a platter and serve hot.

Chinese Broccoli with Oyster Sauce (Ho Yeow Gai Lan)

Prep time: 5 minutes |Cook time: 5 minutes |Serves 4

- ¼ cup oyster sauce
- 2 teaspoons light soy sauce
- 1 teaspoon sesame oil
- 2 tablespoons cooking oil
- 4 peeled fresh ginger slices, each about the size of a quarter
- 4 garlic cloves, peeled
- Kosher salt
- 2 bunches gai lan (Chinese broccoli), tough ends trimmed
- 2 tablespoons water

1. In a small bowl, stir together the oyster sauce, soy sauce, and sesame oil and set aside.
2. In the wok, heat the cooking oil over medium-high heat until it shimmers. Add the ginger, garlic, and a pinch of salt. Allow the aromatics to sizzle in the oil, swirling gently for about 10 seconds.
3. Add the gai lan and stir, tossing until coated with oil and bright green. Add the water and cover to steam the gai lan for about 3 minutes, or until the stalks can easily be pierced with a knife. Remove the ginger and garlic and discard.
4. Stir in the sauce and toss to coat until hot. Transfer to a serving plate.

Sichuan Two-Potato Stir-fry

Prep time: 15 minutes |Cook time: 10 minutes |Serves 4

- 3 tablespoons cooking oil
- 1 tablespoon chopped fresh ginger
- 4 garlic cloves, crushed and chopped
- 1 large sweet potato, julienned into matchstick pieces (2 cups)
- 1 large white potato, julienned into matchstick pieces (2 cups)
- 1 tablespoon red pepper flakes
- 1 tablespoon Chinese five spice powder
- ½ teaspoon ground Sichuan peppercorns
- 1 teaspoon spicy sesame oil
- 4 scallions, both white and green parts, julienned into matchstick pieces
- Rice or noodles, for serving

1. In the wok, heat the cooking oil over high heat until it shimmers.
2. Add the ginger, garlic, sweet potato, and white potato and Stir-fry for 2 minutes, until the potatoes are lightly browned.
3. Sprinkle in the red pepper flakes and five-spice powder and Stir-fry for 1 minute, until fragrant.
4. Add the Sichuan peppercorns, spicy sesame oil, and scallions and Stir-fry for 1 minute. Serve over rice or noodles.

Steamed Baby Bok Choy with Garlic and Hoisin Sauce
Prep time: 5 minutes |Cook time: 5 minutes |Serves 4

- 8 baby bok choy heads, trimmed and cut in half lengthwise
- ¼ cup hoisin sauce
- 1 teaspoon avocado oil
- 2 cloves of garlic, chopped

1. In a pie pan or shallow dish, arrange the bok choy halves, cut-side up.
2. Coat the bok choy lightly with the hoisin sauce.
3. In the wok, bring 1 inch of water to a boil over high heat. Place a rack in the wok and the pan on the rack. Cover and steam for 4 minutes, until tender-crisp.
4. Remove the bok choy and the rack from the wok. Add the oil to the wok and heat over medium heat until it shimmers.
5. Add the chopped garlic and Stir-fryfor 1 minute or until golden brown.
6. Sprinkle the steamed bok choy with the fried garlic and serve as a side dish.

Steamed Chinese Broccoli with Tahini
Prep time: 10 minutes |Cook time: 10 minutes |Serves 4

- 2 tablespoons tahini
- 2 tablespoons Shaoxing cooking wine
- 2 tablespoons dark soy sauce
- 1 tablespoon toasted sesame oil
- 1 pound gai lan (Chinese broccoli), cut diagonally into 2-inch pieces, discarding first inch of stems

1. In a bowl, whisk the tahini, wine, soy sauce, and sesame oil together.
2. Toss the sliced gai lan with the sauce and arrange it in a pie pan or shallow dish.
3. Heat 1 inch of water over high heat in the wok. Place a rack in the wok and the pie pan on the rack.
4. Cover and steam the gai lan for 3 or 4 minutes, until tender-crisp.
5. Toss the steamed gai lan to recoat the pieces with sauce. Serve as a side by itself, or over rice and noodles.

Hot and Sour Stir-fry Vegetables
Prep time: 10 minutes |Cook time: 5 minutes |Serves 4

- 2 tablespoons avocado oil
- 1 tablespoon ginger root, crushed and chopped
- 2 cloves garlic, crushed and chopped
- 1 medium carrot roll cut into ½-inch pieces (1 cup)
- 1 medium yellow onion diced into 1-inch pieces
- 1 tablespoon dried crushed red pepper flakes
- 1 teaspoon spicy sesame oil
- 2 cups sugar snap or snow pea pods
- 4 ounces fresh shiitake mushrooms sliced into ¼-inch pieces
- 2 tablespoons black Chinese rice vinegar
- Grated zest of 1 lemon
- 2 tablespoons fresh lemon juice (1 lemon)
- 2 tablespoons thick soy sauce
- 1 tablespoon sesame seeds
- 4 scallions sliced diagonally into ¼-inch pieces

1. In the wok, heat the oil over high heat until it shimmers.
2. Add the ginger, garlic, and carrot to the wok and Stir-fryfor 1 minute.
3. Add the onion and red pepper flakes to the wok and Stir-fryfor 1 minute.
4. Add the spicy sesame oil, pea pods, and mushrooms to the wok and Stir-fryfor 1 minute.
5. Add the vinegar, lemon zest and juice, and thick soy sauce to the wok and Stir-fryfor 30 seconds or until a light glaze is formed.
6. Toss in sesame seeds and scallions and serve over rice or noodles.

Green Beans, Carrot, Red Peppers, Corn and Snow Peas Stir Fry
Prep time: 5 minutes | Cook time: 10 minutes| Serves 2

- 1/2 cup sliced green beans
- 1/2 cup sliced snow peas
  1 cup cubed tofu
- 1/2 cup sliced red peppers
- 1/2 cup shredded carrots
- 1/2 cup corn
- 1/2 cup sliced onions
- 1 Tbsp. oil

1. Marinade tofu in Superfoods marinade.
2. Stir-frydrained tofu in coconut oil for few minutes, add all vegetables and Stir-fryfor 2 more minutes.
3. Add the rest of the marinade and Stir-fryfor a minute. Serve with brown rice or quinoa.

Stir-Fried Cucumbers and Spicy Peanut Sauce
Prep time: 10 minutes |Cook time: 10 minutes |Serves 4

- ¼ cup peanut butter
- 2 tablespoons light soy sauce
- 1 tablespoon sriracha sauce
- 1 tablespoon spicy sesame oil
- 1 tablespoon brown sugar
- 2 tablespoons cooking oil
- 2 European cucumbers, roll-cut into 1-inch pieces (no need to peel or remove seeds)
- 1 tablespoon toasted sesame seeds, for garnishing

1. In a bowl, whisk together the peanut butter, soy sauce, sriracha, sesame oil, and brown sugar until smooth.
2. In the wok, heat the cooking oil over high heat until it shimmers.
3. Add the cucumbers and Stir-fryfor 2 minutes, until the cucumbers are tender.
4. Pour in the sauce and Stir-fryfor 1 minute to mix well.
5. Garnish with sesame seeds and serve as a side dish.

Stir-Fried Broccoli and Straw Mushrooms in Brown Sauce
Prep time: 10 minutes |Cook time: 10 minutes |Serves 4

- ¼ cup water
- 3 tablespoons Shaoxing cooking wine
- 3 tablespoons light soy sauce
- 1 tablespoon brown sugar
- 1 tablespoon cornstarch
- 2 tablespoons cooking oil
- 1 tablespoon chopped fresh ginger
- 3 garlic cloves, crushed and chopped
- 2 cups broccoli florets cut into 1-inch pieces
- 1 medium onion, cut into 1-inch pieces
- 1 (15-ounce) can straw mushrooms, drained and rinsed
- 4 scallions, both white and green parts, cut into ¼-inch pieces
- Rice or noodles, for serving

1. In a small bowl, combine the water, wine, soy sauce, brown sugar, and cornstarch and set aside.
2. In the wok, heat the oil over high heat until it shimmers.
3. Add the ginger, garlic, and broccoli and Stir-fryfor 2 minutes, until the broccoli is bright green.
4. Add the onion and Stir-fryfor 1 minute.
5. Add the mushrooms and Stir-fryfor 1 minute.
6. Give the cornstarch mixture a stir and gradually pour it into the wok, stirring constantly until a light glaze is formed. For a thinner glaze, add water a tablespoon at a time.
7. Toss in the scallions and serve over rice or noodles

Calamari and Green Peas Stir Fry
Prep time: 5 minutes | Cook time: 10 minutes| Serves 2

- 1/2 pound calamari (squid rings)
  2 cups green peas
- 1/2 cup sliced onions
- 1 Tbsp. coconut oil

1. Marinade calamari in a Superfoods marinade.
2. Stir-frydrained calamari and green peas in coconut oil for few minutes, add onions and Stir-fryfor 2 more minutes.
3. Add the rest of the marinade and Stir-fryfor a minute.
4. Serve with brown rice or quinoa.

Broccoli, Green Onions and Red Peppers Stir-fry
Prep time: 5 minutes | Cook time: 10 minutes| Serves 2

- 1/2 pound broccoli, with stalks peeled
  1 cup red peppers
- 1 cup green onions
- 1 Tbsp. coconut oil

1. Marinade peeled and sliced broccoli stalks in a Superfoods marinade.
2. Stir-frydrained broccoli stalks, broccoli florets and red peppers in coconut oil for 4-5 more minutes.
3. Add the rest of the marinade, green onions and Stir-fryfor a minute.
4. Serve with brown rice or quinoa.

Kale and Mushrooms Stir-fry
Prep time: 5 minutes | Cook time: 10 minutes| Serves 2

- 1/2-pound shiitake and Portobello mushrooms
  2 cups Kale
- 1/2 cup sliced onions
- 1 Tbsp. coconut oil

1. Marinade shiitake in a Superfoods marinade.
2. Stir-frydrained shiitake and kale in coconut oil for few minutes, add all other vegetables and Stir-fryfor 2 more minutes.
3. Add the rest of the marinade and Stir-fryfor a minute.
4. Serve with brown rice or quinoa.

Kale, Carrot and Green Peas Stir-fry

Prep time: 5 minutes | Cook time: 10 minutes| Serves 2

- 1/2 pound green peas
  2 cups kale
- 1/2 cup sliced carrots
- 1/2 cup onion
- 1 Tbsp. coconut oil

1. Marinade green peas in a Superfoods marinade.
2. Stir-fry drained green peas and kale in coconut oil for few minutes, add all vegetables and Stir-fry for 2 more minutes.
3. Add the rest of the marinade and Stir-fry for a minute.
4. Serve with brown rice or quinoa.

Fennel, Bok Choy, Red Pepper and Celery Stir-fry

Prep time: 5 minutes | Cook time: 10 minutes| Serves 2

- 1 cup sliced celery
  1 cup sliced fennel bulb
- 1/2 cup sliced red peppers
- 1 cup sliced bok choy
- 1 Tbsp. coconut oil

1. Marinade fennel in a Superfoods marinade.
2. Stir-fry drained fennel and celery in coconut oil for 4-5 more minutes.
3. Add the rest of the marinade, bok choy and red peppers and Stir-fry for a minute.
4. Serve with brown rice or quinoa.

Okra, Sprouts and Onions Choy Stir-fry

Prep time: 5 minutes | Cook time: 10 minutes| Serves 2

- 1 + 1/2 pound sliced okra
  1 cup sprouts
- 1/2 cup sliced onions
- 1 Tbsp. coconut oil

1. Marinade okra in a Superfoods marinade.
2. Stir-fry drained okra in coconut oil for few minutes, add onions and Stir-fry for 2 more minutes.
3. Add the rest of the marinade and sprouts and Stir-fry for a minute.
4. Serve with brown rice or quinoa.

Sesame with Japanese Stir-Fried Vegetables

Prep time: 10 minutes | Cook time: 3½ minutes | Serves 4

- 2 tablespoons yellow miso
- 2 tablespoons mirin
- 2 tablespoons tamari
- 1 tablespoon toasted sesame oil
- 2 tablespoons cooking oil
- 1 tablespoon crushed, chopped ginger
- 2 garlic cloves, crushed and chopped
- 1 medium carrot, roll-cut into ½-inch pieces
- 1 medium onion, cut into 1-inch pieces
- 4 ounces shiitake mushrooms, cut into slices
- 1 red bell pepper, cut into 1-inch pieces
- 4 scallions, cut into 1-inch pieces
- 2 cups bean sprouts

1. In a small bowl, whisk together the miso, mirin, tamari, and sesame oil. Set aside.
2. In a wok over high heat, heat the cooking oil until it shimmers.
3. Add the ginger, garlic, and carrot and Stir-fry for 1 minute.
4. Add the onion and mushrooms and Stir-fry for 1 minute.
5. Add the bell pepper and scallions and Stir-fry for 1 minute.
6. Add the miso mixture and toss for 30 seconds.
7. Serve with steamed Japanese rice and garnish with bean sprouts.

Soy Sauce with Filipino Vegetables

Prep time: 10 minutes | Cook time: 4 minutes | Serves 4

- 2 tablespoons cooking oil
- 2 garlic cloves, crushed and chopped
- 1 tablespoon crushed, chopped ginger
- 1 medium carrot, roll-cut into ½-inch pieces
- 1 medium onion, diced
- 12 cherry tomatoes, cut in half
- 2 cups sugar snap or snow pea pods
- 1 red bell pepper, cut into 1-inch pieces
- ¼ cup oyster sauce
- 2 tablespoons soy sauce

1. In a wok over high heat, heat the cooking oil until it shimmers.
2. Add the garlic, ginger, and carrot and Stir-fry for 1 minute.
3. Add the onion and Stir-fry for 1 minute.
4. Add the cherry tomatoes and Stir-fry for 1 minute.
5. Add the pea pods and bell pepper and Stir-fry for 1 minute.
6. Add the oyster sauce and soy sauce and stir until a light glaze forms.
7. Serve over steamed rice.

Spicy Kimchi with Korean Vegetables

Prep time: 10 minutes | Cook time: 5 minutes | Serve 4

- 2 tablespoons cooking oil
- 1 tablespoon crushed, chopped ginger
- 2 garlic cloves, crushed and chopped
- 1 medium onion, cut into 1-inch pieces
- 4 ounces shiitake mushrooms, sliced
- 2 cups sugar snap or snow pea pods
- 1 red bell pepper, cut into 1-inch pieces
- 2 heads baby bok choy, leaves separated
- 2 tablespoons gochujang
- ½ cup kimchi
- 2 tablespoons soy sauce

1. In a wok over high heat, heat the cooking oil until it shimmers.
2. Add the ginger, garlic, and onion and Stir-fryfor 1 minute.
3. Add the mushrooms and Stir-fryfor 1 minute.
4. Add the pea pods and Stir-fryfor 1 minute.
5. Add the bell pepper and bok choy and Stir-fryfor 1 minute.
6. Add the gochujang, kimchi, and soy sauce and Stir-fryfor 1 minute.
7. Serve over steamed jasmine rice.

Spicy Malaysian Vegetable Curry

Prep time: 10 minutes | Cook time: 5 minutes | Serve 4

- 2 tablespoons soy sauce
- 1 tablespoon hot sesame oil
- 1 teaspoon Chinese five spice powder
- ¼ teaspoon ground cumin
- ¼ teaspoon ground fennel
- ½ teaspoon ground chili powder
- 2 tablespoons coconut oil
- 1 tablespoon crushed, chopped ginger
- 1 medium carrot, roll-cut into ½-inch pieces
- 1 medium red onion, diced
- 2 cups sugar snap or snow pea pods
- ¼ cup unsweetened and shredded dried coconut

1. In a small bowl, whisk together the soy sauce, sesame oil, five-spice powder, cumin, fennel, and chili powder. Set aside.
2. In a wok over high heat, heat the coconut oil until it shimmers.
3. Add the ginger and carrot and Stir-fryfor 1 minute.
4. Add the onion and Stir-fryfor 1 minute.
5. Add the pea pods and the soy sauce mixture and Stir-fryfor 1 minute.
6. Add the coconut and Stir-fryfor 1 minute.
7. Serve over steamed rice made with coconut water or coconut milk.

Limey Carrot with Spiced Vegetable

Prep time: 10 minutes | Cook time: 4½ minutes | Serve 4

- 1 teaspoon hot sesame oil
- Juice of 1 lime
- 1 tablespoon fish sauce
- 1 tablespoon Chinese five spice powder
- 2 tablespoons cooking oil
- 2 garlic cloves, crushed and chopped
- 1 medium carrot, roll-cut into ½-inch pieces
- 2 to 3 red chiles, cut into ¼-inch pieces
- 2 cups sugar snap or snow pea pods
- 1 red bell pepper, cut into 1-inch pieces
- 1 small mango, peeled and cut into ½-inch pieces
- 2 baby bok choy, leaves separated

1. In a small bowl, whisk together the sesame oil, lime juice, fish sauce, and five-spice powder. Set aside.
2. In a wok over high heat, heat the cooking oil until it shimmers.
3. Add the garlic and carrot and Stir-fryfor 1 minute.
4. Add the chiles and Stir-fryfor 30 seconds.
5. Add the pea pods and bell pepper and Stir-fryfor 1 minute.
6. Add the mango and Stir-fryfor 1 minute, then add the sesame oil mixture.
7. Add the bok choy and Stir-fryfor 1 minute.
8. Serve over steamed jasmine rice.

Chapter 10
Noodle and Fried Rice Dishes

Shrimp Fried Rice
Prep time: 5 minutes | Cook time: 10 minutes| Serves 4

- 2 tablespoons cooking oil
- 1 tablespoon crushed, chopped ginger
- 2 garlic cloves, crushed and chopped
- ½ teaspoon kosher salt
- 2 large eggs, beaten
- 1 medium onion, diced
- ½ pound medium shrimp, peeled, deveined, and halved lengthwise
- 1 cup frozen peas, thawed
- 2 cups cold, cooked rice
- 1 teaspoon sesame oil
- 1 tablespoon soy sauce
- 4 scallions, cut into ½-inch pieces

1. In a wok over high heat, heat the cooking oil until it shimmers.
2. Add the ginger, garlic, salt, and eggs and Stir-fry-for 1 minute, or until the eggs are firm.
3. Add the onion and shrimp and Stir-fryfor 1 minute.
4. Add the peas, rice, sesame oil, and soy sauce and Stir-fryfor 1 minute.
5. Garnish with the scallions and serve immediately.

Vegetable Fried Rice
Prep time: 5 minutes | Cook time: 10 minutes| Serves 4

- 2 tablespoons cooking oil
- 1 tablespoon crushed, chopped ginger
- 2 garlic cloves, crushed and chopped
- ½ teaspoon kosher salt
- 4 large eggs, beaten
- 1 medium carrot, julienned
- 1 medium onion, diced
- 1 red bell pepper, diced
- 1 cup frozen peas, thawed
- 2 cups cold, cooked rice
- 1 teaspoon sesame oil
- 1 tablespoon soy sauce
- 4 scallions, cut into ½-inch pieces

1. In a wok over high heat, heat the cooking oil until it shimmers.
2. Add the ginger, garlic, salt, and eggs and Stir-fry-for 1 minute, or until the eggs are firm.
3. Add the carrot and Stir-fryfor 1 minute.
4. Add the onion and Stir-fryfor 1 minute.
5. Add the bell pepper and Stir-fryfor 1 minute.
6. Add the peas, rice, sesame oil, and soy sauce and Stir-fryfor 1 minute.
7. Garnish with the scallions and serve immediately.

Kimchi Fried Rice
Prep time: 5 minutes | Cook time: 10 minutes| Serves 4

- ½ pound thick-sliced bacon, cut into 1-inch pieces
- 1 tablespoon crushed, chopped ginger
- 2 garlic cloves, crushed and chopped
- 4 ounces sliced mushrooms
- 1 cup kimchi, cut into ½-inch pieces
- 2 cups cold, cooked rice
- 1 teaspoon sesame oil
- 4 scallions, cut into ½-inch pieces
- 1 tablespoon soy sauce
- ¼ cup kimchi juice
- 4 large eggs

1. Place the bacon, ginger, and garlic in a wok over high heat and Stir-fryfor 2 minutes, or until the bacon is lightly browned.
2. Drain off all but 2 tablespoons of the bacon fat from the wok and set aside.
3. Add the mushrooms to the wok and Stir-fryfor 1 minute.
4. Add the kimchi and Stir-fryfor 30 seconds.
5. Add the rice, sesame oil, scallions, soy sauce, and kimchi juice. Stir-fryfor 30 seconds, then remove from the wok and place on a serving dish.
6. Return 2 tablespoons of the reserved bacon fat to the wok and fry the eggs sunny-side up.
7. Serve the rice with the fried eggs on top.

Indonesian Fried Rice (Nasi Goreng)
Prep time: 5 minutes | Cook time: 10 minutes| Serves 4

- 3 tablespoons cooking oil, divided
- ½ pound ground meat of your choice
- 1 tablespoon crushed, chopped ginger
- 2 garlic cloves, crushed and chopped
- 1 medium onion, diced
- 2 cups cold, cooked rice
- ¼ cup kecap manis
- 1 teaspoon hot sesame oil
- 4 scallions, cut into ½-inch pieces
- 4 eggs
- 2 tomatoes, sliced
- 1 cucumber, sliced

1. In a wok over high heat, heat 2 tablespoons of the cooking oil until it shimmers.
2. Add the meat, ginger, garlic, and onion and Stir-fryfor 1 minute.
3. Add the rice, kecap manis, sesame oil, and scallions and Stir-fryfor 1 minute. Remove from the wok and place in a serving bowl.
4. Add the remaining 1 tablespoon of cooking oil to the wok and, when the oil is shimmering, fry the eggs sunny-side up.
5. Serve each portion of rice with a fried egg on top, and sliced tomatoes and cucumbers on the side.

Classic Vietnamese Pho
Prep time: 15 minutes | Cook time: 5 hours | Serves 6

- 2 (3-inch) pieces ginger, cut in half lengthwise
- 2 onions, peeled
- 5 pounds (2.3 kg) beef marrow
- 2 pounds (907 g) beef chuck, cut into 2 pieces
- 2 scallions, cut into 4-inch lengths
- ⅓ cup fish sauce
- 2½ ounces rock sugar
- 8-star anise
- 6 cloves
- 1 cinnamon stick
- 1 black cardamom pod
- 2 teaspoons fennel seeds
- 2 teaspoons coriander seeds
- 1 tablespoon salt
- 1 pound (454 g) dried pho noodles, boiled
- ⅓ pound (151 g) beef sirloin, sliced

1. Sauté onions and ginger with oil in a large wok for 5 minutes.
2. Stir in meat and beef marrow then cover to cook for 40 minutes.
3. Toast all the whole spices in a dry skillet for 3 minutes then seal the spices in a spice infuser.
4. Place the spice infuser to the broth and cover to cook for 4 hours.
5. Stir in sugar, salt, and fish sauce, then mix well.
6. Remove the spice infuser from the soup.
7. Add remaining including noodles then cook for 5 minutes.
8. Serve warm.

Garlic Asian Noodles
Prep time: 10 minutes | Cook time: 1 minutes | Serves 6

- 12 ounces (340 g) thin spaghetti
- 4 tablespoons unsalted butter
- 8 garlic cloves, peeled and sliced
- ⅛ teaspoon turmeric
- 1 tablespoon oyster sauce
- 1 tablespoon soy sauce
- 1 to 2 teaspoons brown sugar
- 1 teaspoon sesame oil
- 1 to 2 whole scallions, chopped
- ¼ cup Parmesan cheese

1. Boil the spaghetti in hot water as per package's instructions then drain.
2. Sauté garlic with butter in a Cantonese wok oven for 30 seconds.
3. Mix turmeric, soy sauce, oyster sauce, brown sugar, sesame oil, scallions, and Parmesan cheese in a bowl.
4. Pour this mixture into the wok and cook for 30 seconds.
5. Toss in boiled spaghetti and mix well with the sauce.
6. Serve warm.

Indian Fried Rice (Fodni Bhaat)
Prep time: 5 minutes | Cook time: 8 minutes| Serves 4

- 2 tablespoons cooking oil
- 1 tablespoon crushed, chopped ginger
- 1 medium onion, diced
- 1 teaspoon mustard seeds
- 2 garlic cloves, crushed and chopped
- 2 bird's eye chiles, sliced into ¼-inch circles
- 1 teaspoon hot sesame oil
- ½ teaspoon turmeric
- ½ teaspoon ground coriander
- ¼ teaspoon kosher salt
- 2 cups cold, cooked basmati rice
- ¼ cup coarsely chopped mint leaves

1. In a wok over high heat, heat the cooking oil until it shimmers.
2. Add the ginger, onion, mustard seeds, and garlic to the wok and Stir-fryfor 1 minute.
3. Add the bird's eye chiles, sesame oil, turmeric, coriander, salt, and rice and Stir-fryfor 1 minute.
4. Garnish with the mint and serve immediately.

Chili Singapore Noodles with Stock
Prep time: 15 minutes | Cook time: 7½ minutes | Serves 6

- 5 ounces (142 g) dried vermicelli rice noodles
- 12 large frozen shrimp; peeled, deveined, and butterflied
- 2½ tablespoons vegetable oil
- 2 eggs, beaten
- 2 garlic cloves, chopped
- 4 ounces (113 g) char Siu, Chinese Roast Pork
- 3 dried red chili peppers
- 9 ounces (255 g) Napa cabbage, shredded
- 1 medium carrot
- 1 tablespoon Shaoxing wine
- 2 tablespoons curry powder
- 2 teaspoons salt
- ¼ teaspoon sugar
- ⅛ teaspoon white pepper
- 2 to 4 tablespoons chicken stock
- 1 tablespoon vegetable oil
- ½ teaspoon sesame oil
- 1½ teaspoons soy sauce
- 1 scallion, julienned
- ½ cored onion, thinly sliced

1. Boil the dry noodles in hot water as per package's instructions then drain.
2. Sauté garlic with oil in a Cantonese wok for 30 seconds.
3. Stir in cabbage, carrot, and onion, then sauté for 5 minutes.
4. Add shrimp and rest of the ingredients(except the noodles).
5. Cover and cook for 2 minutes until shrimp turn white.
6. Stir in noodles and mix well.
7. Serve warm.

Egg with Fried Brown Rice
Prep time: 15 minutes | Cook time: 15 minutes | Serves 8

- 4 cups cooked brown rice
- 8 ounces (227 g) beef, chicken, or pork, cut into ½-inch pieces
- 1 tablespoon water
- 1½ teaspoon dark mushroom soy sauce
- 1 teaspoon vegetable oil
- 1 teaspoon cornstarch
- ¼ teaspoon granulated sugar
- ⅛ teaspoon ground white pepper
- ½ teaspoon sesame oil
- 1 teaspoon dark soy sauce
- 1 tablespoon light soy sauce
- 3 tablespoons vegetable oil
- 2 eggs, beaten
- 1 medium onion, chopped
- ¾ cup carrots, chopped
- 1 tablespoon Shaoxing wine
- 1 cup frozen peas
- 1 scallion, chopped

1. Beat eggs with salt and wine in a bowl.
2. Pour this mixture into a greased wok and stir cook for 1 minute. Transfer it to a plate.
3. Mix cornstarch with water, soy sauce, white pepper, and sesame oil in a bowl.
4. Sauté onion, carrot, and peas with oil in a cooking pot for 5 minutes.
5. Stir in meat then sauté for 7 minutes.
6. Pour in prepared sauce and mix well.
7. Add cooked eggs, rice, wine, and scallions, then mix well to cook for 2 minutes.
8. Serve warm.

Japanese Fried Rice (Yakimeshi)
Prep time: 5 minutes | Cook time: 8 minutes | Serves 4

- ½ pound thick-sliced bacon, cut into 1-inch pieces
- 1 tablespoon crushed, chopped ginger
- 2 garlic cloves, crushed and chopped
- 3 eggs, beaten
- 2 cups cold, cooked rice
- 1 teaspoon sesame oil
- 4 scallions, cut into ½-inch pieces
- 2 tablespoons sesame seeds
- Kosher salt
- Ground black pepper

1. In a wok over high heat, Stir-fry the bacon, ginger, and garlic for 2 minutes, or until the bacon is lightly browned.
2. Remove the bacon and set aside.
3. Add the eggs and Stir-fry until they are firm and dry.
4. Add the cooked bacon, rice, and sesame oil and Stir-fry for 1 minute.
5. Add the scallions and sesame seeds and toss for 30 seconds.
6. Serve with salt and pepper to taste.

Pork Pad Mee Kati
Prep time: 25 Minutes | Cook time: 5 Minutes | Serves 4

- 8 ounces thin rice noodles
- 2 tablespoons cooking oil
- 4 garlic cloves, crushed and chopped
- 1 tablespoon crushed and chopped ginger
- 1 pound ground pork
- 1 tablespoon red Thai curry paste
- Juice and zest of 1 lime
- ¼ cup pad Thai sauce
- 1 (14-ounce) can coconut milk
- 4 large eggs, scrambled
- 2 cups fresh bean sprouts
- 2 cups basil leaves
- 6 scallions, cut diagonally into ½-inch pieces
- ¼ cup cilantro leaves, coarsely chopped
- ½ cup coarsely chopped peanuts
- 1 lime, cut into wedges, for serving

1. Cover the rice noodles in a large bowl of hot tap water while preparing the rest of the ingredients. There is no need to drain or rinse until you're ready to serve.
2. In a wok, heat the cooking oil over high heat until it begins to smoke.
3. Add the garlic, ginger, pork, and curry paste to the wok and Stir-fry for 1 minute.
4. Add the lime juice, lime zest, and pad Thai sauce to the wok and Stir-fry for 1 minute.
5. Add the coconut milk and bring to a simmer.
6. Drizzle the scrambled eggs into the boiling broth while stirring slowly to form threads of poached egg in the broth.
7. Divide the noodles, bean sprouts, basil leaves, and scallions among four soup bowls.
8. Ladle hot broth, eggs, and pork into each bowl. Garnish with the cilantro and peanuts. Serve immediately with lime wedges.

Beef Bulgogi Japchae
Prep time: 25 Minutes | Cook time: 5 Minutes | Serves 4

- 8 ounces dried glass noodles
- ½ pound sirloin steak, cut into ¼-inch strips across the grain
- 2 tablespoons Shaoxing wine
- 1 teaspoon sesame oil
- 1 tablespoon brown sugar
- 2 tablespoons cooking oil
- 4 garlic cloves, crushed and chopped
- 1 tablespoon crushed and chopped ginger
- 1 cup carrots, julienned
- 4 ounces sliced shiitake mushrooms
- ¼ cup thick soy sauce
- 2 cups coarsely chopped spinach
- 4 scallions, cut diagonally into ¼-inch pieces
- 1 tablespoon sesame seeds

1. While prepping the vegetables and meat, soak the glass noodles in hot water for 10 to 20 minutes, until softened.
2. Combine the steak, wine, sesame oil, and sugar in a 2-cup bowl.
3. In a wok, heat the cooking oil over high heat until it begins to smoke.
4. Add the garlic, ginger, carrots, and steak to the wok and Stir-fry for 1 minute.
5. Add the mushrooms and Stir-fry for 1 minute.
6. Add the noodles and Stir-fry for 1 minute.
7. Add the thick soy sauce and spinach and Stir-fry for 1 minute.
8. Add the scallions and sesame seeds, toss, and serve.

Honey Pork Fried Rice
Prep time: 15 minutes | Cook time: 12 minutes | Serves 6

- 1 tablespoon hot water
- 1 teaspoon honey
- 1 teaspoon sesame oil
- 1 teaspoon Shaoxing wine
- 1 tablespoon soy sauce
- 1 teaspoon dark soy sauce
- ¼ teaspoon white pepper
- 5 cups cooked Jasmine rice
- 1 tablespoon oil
- 1 medium onion, diced
- 1 pound (454 g) Chinese BBQ pork, cut into ½-inch chunks
- 1 teaspoon salt
- ½ cup bean sprouts
- 2 eggs, scrambled
- 2 scallions, chopped

1. Sauté onion, bean sprouts, and pork with oil in a Mandarin wok for 7 minutes.
2. Stir in rest of the ingredients along with eggs (except rice).
3. Mix well and cook for 5 minutes.
4. Stir in rice and mix gently.
5. Serve warm.

Chicken Pad Thai
Prep time: 25 Minutes | Cook time: 5 Minutes | Serves 4

- 8 ounces dried rice noodles
- 2 quarts water
- 2 tablespoons cooking oil
- 1 tablespoon crushed and chopped ginger
- 2 garlic cloves, crushed and chopped
- 2 large eggs, beaten
- 1 pound boneless chicken thighs, cut into 1-inch pieces across the grain
- 2 bird's eye peppers, cut into ¼-inch pieces
- ¼ cup pad Thai sauce
- ½ cup chopped peanuts
- 1 cup bean sprouts
- ½ cup coarsely chopped cilantro
- 1 lime, cut into wedges

1. Prepare the dried rice noodles by bringing the water to a boil and then turning the heat off. Place the noodles in the pot and stir for 1 minute, until the noodles are flexible. Let the noodles soak for 2 to 3 minutes, until the noodles are al dente, cooked but firm. Drain and set them aside.
2. Add the chicken and peppers and Stir-fry for 1 minute.
3. Add the pad Thai sauce and Stir-fry for 1 minute.
4. Serve over the cooked rice noodles and garnish with the chopped peanuts, sprouts, cilantro, and lime wedges.

Vegetable Fried Rice with Lapsang Souchong
Prep time: 25 Minutes | Cook time: 5 Minutes | Serves 4

- 2 tablespoons cooking oil
- 2 garlic cloves, crushed and chopped
- 1 tablespoon crushed and chopped ginger
- 4 large eggs, scrambled
- 4 ounces shiitake mushrooms, sliced
- 1 medium red onion, diced into ¼-inch pieces
- 2 cups cooked day-old rice, cooked in lapsang souchong tea
- 1 tablespoon soy sauce
- 1 teaspoon toasted sesame oil
- 1 cup frozen carrots, thawed
- 1 cup frozen peas, thawed
- 1 tablespoon sesame seeds
- 4 scallions, cut diagonally into ¼-inch pieces

1. In a wok, heat the cooking oil over high heat until it begins to smoke.
2. Add the garlic, ginger, and eggs to the wok and Stir-fry for 1 minute, or until the eggs are dry.
3. Add the mushrooms and Stir-fry for 1 minute.
4. Add the onion, rice, soy sauce, and sesame oil and Stir-fry for 1 minute.
5. Add the carrots, peas, and sesame seeds and Stir-fry for 1 minute, or until all the ingredients are well combined.
6. Add the scallions, toss, and serve.

Beef and Mushroom Saffron Fried Rice

Prep time: 25 Minutes | Cook time: 5 Minutes| Serves 4

- 2 tablespoons Shaoxing rice wine
- 12 saffron threads (about 3 per person)
- 2 tablespoons cooking oil
- 1 tablespoon crushed and chopped ginger
- 2 garlic cloves, crushed and chopped
- 15 ounces straw mushrooms, drained and rinsed
- 4 large eggs, scrambled
- ½ pound ground beef
- 1 medium onion, diced into ½-inch pieces
- 1 red bell pepper, diced into ½-inch pieces
- ½ teaspoon salt
- 2 cups cooked day-old rice
- 1 tablespoon soy sauce
- 1 teaspoon toasted sesame oil
- 4 scallions, cut diagonally into ¼-inch pieces

1. Pour the wine into a small bowl, glass, or jar. Crumble the saffron into the wine and set it aside to soak.
2. In a wok, heat the cooking oil over high heat until it begins to smoke.
3. Add the ginger, garlic, mushrooms, and eggs and Stir-fryfor 2 minutes, or until the eggs are cooked.
4. Add the ground beef, onion, bell pepper, salt, and black pepper and Stir-fryfor 1 minute.
5. Add the rice, soy sauce, saffron-infused wine, and sesame oil and Stir-fryfor 1 minute, or until all the ingredients are well combined.
6. Add the scallions, toss, and serve.

Yangzhou Fried Rice with Chinese Sausage

Prep time: 25 Minutes | Cook time: 5 Minutes| Serves 4

- 2 tablespoons cooking oil
- 2 garlic cloves, crushed and chopped
- 1 tablespoon crushed and chopped ginger
- 4 large eggs, scrambled
- ¼ pound lap cheong (about 2 or 3 links), cut diagonally into ⅛-inch pieces
- 1 medium onion, diced into ½-inch pieces
- 1 red bell pepper, diced into ½-inch pieces
- ½ teaspoon salt
- ½ teaspoon black or white pepper
- 2 cups cooked day-old rice
- 1 tablespoon soy sauce
- 1 teaspoon toasted sesame oil
- 4 scallions, cut diagonally into ¼-inch pieces

1. In a wok, heat the cooking oil over high heat until it begins to smoke.
2. Add the garlic, ginger, eggs, and lap cheong to the wok and Stir-fryfor 2 minutes, or until the eggs are cooked.
3. Add the onion, bell pepper, salt, and black pepper to the wok and Stir-fryfor 1 minute, or until the vegetables are lightly coated with oil.
4. Add the rice, soy sauce, and sesame oil to the wok and Stir-fryfor 1 minute, or until all the ingredients are well combined.
5. Add the scallions, toss, and serve.

Miso Shrimp Fried Rice

Prep time: 25 Minutes | Cook time: 5 Minutes| Serves 4

- 2 tablespoons cooking oil
- 2 garlic cloves, crushed and chopped
- 1 tablespoon crushed and chopped ginger
- 1 medium red onion, diced into ¼-inch pieces
- 4 large eggs, scrambled
- ½ pound large shrimp, shelled, deveined, and sliced in half lengthwise
- ½ teaspoon black or white ground pepper
- 2 cups cooked day-old rice
- 1 tablespoon soy sauce
- 2 tablespoons white miso
- 1 teaspoon toasted sesame oil
- 1 tablespoon sesame seeds

1. In a wok, heat the cooking oil over high heat until it begins to smoke.
2. Add the garlic, ginger, onion, and eggs and Stir-fryfor 2 minutes, or until the eggs are cooked.
3. Add the shrimp, scallions, bell pepper, salt, and black pepper and Stir-fryfor 1 minute, or until the shrimp turns opaque and begins to curl.
4. Add the rice, soy sauce, miso, and sesame oil and Stir-fryfor 1 minute, or until all the ingredients are well combined.
5. Add the sesame seeds, toss, and serve.

Spicey Seafood Lo Mein

Prep time: 15 minutes | Cook time: 3 minutes | Serves 4

- 2 tablespoons cooking oil
- 1 tablespoon crushed, chopped ginger
- 2 garlic cloves, crushed and chopped
- ¼ pound (113 g) ground pork
- 1 medium onion, cut into 1-inch pieces
- 1 red bell pepper, cut into 1-inch pieces
- ¼ pound (113 g) medium shrimp, peeled, deveined, and cut in half lengthwise
- ¼ pound (113 g) sea scallops, cut in half widthwise
- 2 tablespoons soy sauce
- 2 tablespoons rice wine
- ¼ cup oyster sauce
- 1 pound (454 g) cooked noodles

1. In a wok over high heat, heat the cooking oil until it shimmers.
2. Add the ginger, garlic, pork, and onion and Stir-fryfor 1 minute.
3. Add the bell pepper and shrimp and Stir-fryfor 1 minute.
4. Add the scallops and Stir-fryfor 30 seconds.
5. In a small bowl, whisk together the soy sauce, rice wine, and oyster sauce, then add the mixture to the wok.
6. Add the noodles and Stir-fryfor 30 seconds.
7. Serve immediately.

Spicy Mirin Yaki Udon
Prep time: 15 minutes | Cook time: 15½ minutes | Serves 6

- 1 pound (454 g) frozen udon noodles
- 2 tablespoons butter
- 1 garlic clove, minced
- 2 teaspoons dashi powder
- 1 tablespoon oil
- 4 ounces (113 g) pork shoulder
- 4 ounces (113 g) oyster mushrooms, sliced
- 2 tablespoons mirin
- 2 cups cabbage, shredded
- 1 medium carrot, julienned
- ⅛ teaspoon black pepper
- 2 tablespoons soy sauce
- 1 tablespoon water
- 2 scallions, julienned

1. Boil the dry noodles in hot water as per package's instructions then drain.
2. Sauté garlic with butter in a Mandarin wok for 30 seconds.
3. Stir in pork shoulder, then sauté for 5 minutes.
4. Add mushrooms along with remaining except the noodles.
5. Cover and cook for 10 minutes until pork is tender.
6. Stir in noodles and mix well.
7. Serve warm.

Garlicky Asian Noodles
Prep time: 10 minutes | Cook time: 1 minutes | Serves 6

- 12 ounces (340 g) thin spaghetti
- 4 tablespoons unsalted butter
- 8 garlic cloves, peeled and sliced
- ⅛ teaspoon turmeric
- 1 tablespoon oyster sauce
- 1 tablespoon soy sauce
- 1 to 2 teaspoons brown sugar
- 1 teaspoon sesame oil
- 1 to 2 whole scallions, chopped
- ¼ cup Parmesan cheese

1. Boil the spaghetti in hot water as per package's instructions then drain.
2. Sauté garlic with butter in a Cantonese wok oven for 30 seconds.
3. Mix turmeric, soy sauce, oyster sauce, brown sugar, sesame oil, scallions, and Parmesan cheese in a bowl.
4. Pour this mixture into the wok and cook for 30 seconds.
5. Toss in boiled spaghetti and mix well with the sauce.
6. Serve warm.

Chapter 11
Soups

Egg Drop Soup

Serves: 4 | Prep Time: 10 Minutes | Cook Time: 10 Minutes | Serves: 4

- 1½ tablespoons cornstarch
- 3 tablespoons water
- 4 cups Basic Chinese chicken stock, or store bought
- 1 teaspoon salt
- 2 eggs, lightly beaten
- 1 medium tomato, diced
- Pinch ground white pepper
- 1 scallion, chopped

1. In a small bowl, combine the cornstarch and water.
2. In a wok over medium-high heat, bring the chicken stock to a boil. Add the salt.
3. Stir in the cornstarch-water mixture. Return to a boil.
4. Using a pair of chopsticks, swirl the soup, and at the same time slowly pour the beaten eggs into the soup. Swirl faster for a thinner, silky consistency; or slower for a thicker, chunky egg consistency.
5. Add the tomato and pepper, stir, and simmer for 1 minute.
6. Garnish with the scallion, and serve.

Lotus Root with Pork Ribs Soup

Serves 6 To 8 | Prep Time: 10 Minutes | Cook Time: 4 Hours | Serves: 6-8

- 1 pound pork ribs, cut into 1-inch pieces
- 1 pound lotus root, peeled and cut into ¼-inch-thick rounds
- ½ teaspoon peppercorns
- ½ cup dried red dates (optional)
- 12 cups water
- 2 tablespoons soy sauce
- 1 teaspoon salt
- ¼ cup dried goji berries

1. Place the pork ribs, lotus root, peppercorns, red dates (if using), and water in a wok.
2. Simmer over low heat for at least 4 hours, and up to 6 hours.
3. Turn off the heat and add the soy sauce, salt, and goji berries.
4. Allow the soup to sit for about 15 minutes for the goji berries to reconstitute, then serve.

Simple Sour Soup

Serves 6 To 8 | Prep Time: 10 Minutes | Cook Time: 10 Minutes | Serves: 6-8

- 6 cups Basic Chinese chicken stock, or store bought
- 4 tablespoons water
- 2 tablespoons cornstarch
- 2 tablespoons soy sauce
- 1 teaspoon dark soy sauce
- ¼ cup rice vinegar or apple cider vinegar
- 2 teaspoons sesame oil
- 2 teaspoons brown sugar
- 2 pinches ground white pepper
- 2 teaspoons Sichuan chili oil
- ½ cup diced firm tofu
- 4 large shiitake mushrooms, soaked then cut into thin strips
- ½ cup dried wood ear mushrooms, soaked and cut into thin strips
- ¼ cup sliced bamboo shoots
- 2 eggs, lightly beaten

1. In a wok over medium-high heat, bring the chicken stock to a boil.
2. Combine the water and cornstarch in a small bowl and set it aside.
3. Add the soy sauce, dark soy sauce, vinegar, sesame oil, brown sugar, white pepper, and chili oil.
4. Add the tofu, shiitake mushrooms, wood ear mushrooms, and bamboo shoots. Bring to a boil.
5. While stirring, slowly add the cornstarch mixture. Return to a boil.
6. Use chopsticks to stir the soup while slowly pouring the beaten eggs into the soup. The faster you swirl and the faster you pour, the silkier the egg. Swirl and pour slowly for a chunkier egg texture.

Watercress and Pork Soup

Serves 6 To 8 | Prep Time: 10 Minutes | Cook Time: 4 Hours | Serves: 6-8

- 12 cups water, divided
- ½ pound pork ribs or pork shoulder, cut into 1-inch pieces
- 6 to 10 dried red dates
- ¼ cup dried goji berries
- 1 pound watercress
- 1 tablespoon salt
- 3 pinches ground white pepper

1. In a wok, bring 2 cups of water to a boil. Blanch the pork for about 5 minutes. Rinse the pork and the wok, and set the pork aside.
2. In the wok, bring the remaining 10 cups of water to a boil.
3. Return the pork to the wok. Reduce the heat to low and simmer, partially covered, for 3½ hours.
4. Add the red dates, goji berries, watercress, salt, and pepper. Simmer for 10 more minutes, and serve.

Chicken and Sweet Corn Soup

Serves 6 To 8 | Prep Time: 10 Minutes | Cook Time: 10 Minutes| Serves: 6-8

- 2 (14.75-ounce) cans cream-style sweet corn
- 8 cups Basic Chinese chicken stock or store bought
- 2 cups cooked shredded chicken
- 1 teaspoon salt
- 1 teaspoon sesame oil
- 3 teaspoons cornstarch mixed with 2 tablespoons water (optional)
- 2 eggs, lightly beaten
- 1 scallion, chopped

1. In a wok over high heat, add the corn to the chicken stock and bring to a boil.
2. Add the shredded chicken, salt, and sesame oil. Return to a boil.
3. Stir in the cornstarch mixture (if using) to thicken the soup. Return to a boil.
4. Use chopsticks to stir the soup and while stirring, pour the beaten eggs into the soup. The faster you swirl and the faster you pour, the silkier the egg. Swirl and pour slowly for a chunkier egg texture.
5. Garnish with the chopped scallion just before serving.

Sweet Peanut Soup

Serves 4 To 6 | Prep Time: 5 Minutes, Plus 10 To 26 Hours Inactive | Cook Time: 2 Hours| Serves: 4

½ pound raw peanuts, shelled and skinned
1 tablespoon baking soda
8 cups water, plus more for soaking
4 tablespoons sugar

1. Soak the peanuts in a bowl of water overnight.
2. Rinse the peanuts, sprinkle them with the baking soda, then cover in fresh water to soak for 1 to 2 more hours.
3. Thoroughly rinse the peanuts.
4. In a wok over high heat, bring the 8 cups of water to a boil.
5. Add the peanuts to the boiling water, reduce the heat to low, and simmer, partially covered, for 2 hours.
6. Add the sugar in increments until the soup reaches your desired sweetness.
7. Serve the soup at room temperature, hot, or cold, with an almond or butter cookie, if desired.

Cabbage and Pork Meatball Soup

Serves 8 To 10 | Prep Time: 15 Minutes, Plus 15 Minutes To Marinate | Cook Time: 35 Minutes| Serves: 8-10

FOR THE PORK MEATBALLS
- ½ pound ground pork
- ¼ pound minced shrimp (4 to 6 large shrimp)
- ¼ cup finely diced water chestnuts
- 1 teaspoon soy sauce
- ½ teaspoon sugar
- ½ teaspoon salt
- Pinch ground white pepper
- 1½ tablespoons cornstarch
- For the soup
- 10 cups Basic Chinese Chicken Stock, or store bought
- ½ head napa cabbage, cut into 1-inch pieces
- 1 carrot, sliced
- 2 teaspoons salt
- 2 teaspoons sesame oil
- 2 teaspoons soy sauce
- To make the meatballs

1. In a bowl, mix the ground pork, shrimp, water chestnuts, soy sauce, sugar, salt, pepper, and cornstarch. Set aside to marinate for about 15 minutes.

TO MAKE THE SOUP
2. In a wok over high heat, bring the chicken stock to a boil.
3. Add the cabbage and carrot, and simmer for about 30 minutes.
4. Roll about 1 heaping tablespoon of pork mixture into a ball and continue until all the pork mixture is used. Carefully drop the meatballs into the boiling soup one at a time. Avoid stirring. As the meatballs cook, they will rise to the top. They will take about 3 minutes to cook through.
5. Add the salt, sesame oil, and soy sauce just before turning off the heat.

Scallion with Chicken Feet Soup

Prep time: 10 minutes | Cook time: 2¼ hours | Serves 12

- 2 tablespoons dried seaweed, soaked
- 1 cup raw shelled peanuts
- 1½ pounds (680 g) chicken feet
- 2 tablespoons Shaoxing wine
- 4 ginger slices
- 12 cups water
- Salt, to taste
- 1 scallion, chopped

1. Add water, ginger, wine, chicken feet, seaweed, peanuts, and salt in a large wok.
2. Cook the chicken feet soup for 20 minutes, then reduce the heat to low.
3. Continue cooking for 2 hours, then garnish with scallions.
4. Serve warm.

Chinese Mushroom Soup

Serves 6 To 8 | Prep Time: 10 Minutes | Cook Time: 25 Minutes| Serves: 6

- 1 tablespoon olive oil
- ½ onion, sliced
- 2 garlic cloves, minced
- 1 carrot, cut into thin slices
- 4 or 5 large shiitake mushrooms, cut into thin slices
- 5 or 6 white or brown button mushrooms, cut into thin slices
- 1 small bunch enoki mushrooms, roots removed
- 8 cups vegetable stock
- ¼ cup dried goji berries
- 2 teaspoons sesame oil
- 1 tablespoon soy sauce
- 1 teaspoon salt

1. In a wok over medium heat, heat the olive oil.
2. Sauté the onion and garlic until the onion turns slightly translucent.
3. Add the carrot, shiitake mushrooms, button mushrooms, and enoki mushrooms. Sauté for about 1 minute.
4. Pour in the vegetable stock and bring to a boil.
5. Add the goji berries, sesame oil, soy sauce, and salt.
6. Simmer over low heat for about 20 minutes before serving.

Wonton Soup

Serves 6 To 8 | Prep Time: 20 Minutes | Cook Time: 10 Minutes| Serves: 6-8

FOR THE WONTONS

- ¼ pound ground pork
- ¼ pound shrimp, peeled, deveined, and roughly chopped
- 1 teaspoon cornstarch
- 1 teaspoon sesame oil
- 1 teaspoon soy sauce
- ½ teaspoon salt
- Pinch ground white pepper
- 20 to 25 square wonton wrappers
- For the soup
- 8 cups Basic Chinese chicken stock, or store bought
- 2 tablespoons low-sodium soy sauce
- 2 teaspoons sesame oil
- 3 pinches ground white pepper
- 1 scallion, chopped

TO MAKE THE WONTONS

1. In a bowl, mix together the pork, shrimp, cornstarch, sesame oil, soy sauce, salt, and pepper.
2. Place about 1 teaspoon of pork mixture in the center of a wonton wrapper.
3. Dampen your finger with water and run it along the edge of the wonton to help seal it, then fold the wonton in half into a triangle. Gently press the edges to seal.
4. Fold the bottom two corners (just outside the meat

filling) toward each other, and press those corners together to seal them. Set the wontons aside.

TO MAKE THE SOUP

5. Bring the chicken stock to a boil in a wok over high heat. Add the soy sauce and sesame oil.
6. Bring a separate pot of water to a boil. Carefully drop the wontons into the boiling water.
7. As soon as the wontons are cooked, they will float to the top. When they all float to the top, continue boiling for 2 minutes to cook them all the way through.
8. Using a skimmer, carefully transfer the wontons from the water to the chicken stock.
9. Add the pepper and scallion just before serving.

Hot and Sour Soup

Prep time: 20 minutes | Cook time: 11 minutes | Serves 9

- ½ cup lily flowers
- ⅓ ounce (9.6 g) dried wood ear mushrooms, soaked
- ⅔ ounce (19 g) dried shiitake mushrooms, soaked
- 3 ounces (85 g) spiced dry tofu, soaked
- 4 ounces (113 g) fresh firm tofu
- 7 cups vegetable stock
- ½ teaspoon salt
- ¼ teaspoon sugar
- 2 dried red chili peppers, chopped
- 1-2 teaspoons ground white pepper
- 1 ½ teaspoon mushroom dark soy sauce
- 1 tablespoon light soy sauce
- 1 teaspoon sesame oil
- ⅓ cup white vinegar
- 5 ounces (142 g) bamboo shoots
- ¼ cup cornstarch, whisked with ¼ cup water
- 1 large egg, beaten
- 1 scallion, chopped

1. Sauté all the veggies and tofu with cooking oil in a deep wok until golden.
2. Pour in spices, sauces, vinegar, sugar, stock, and lily flowers.
3. Cook the soup for 10 minutes on a simmer.
4. Stir in cornstarch slurry then cook until it thickens.
5. Slowly pour in the egg and cook for 1 minute with a stir.
6. Serve warm.

Mushroom with Vinegary Beef Soup

Prep time: 15 minutes | Cook time: 8 minutes | Serves 4

- 2 tablespoons cooking oil
- 1 tablespoon crushed chopped ginger
- 2 garlic cloves, crushed and chopped
- 1 medium carrot, julienned
- 1 medium onion, cut into 1-inch pieces
- 1 pound (454 g) mushrooms, sliced
- 3 quarts vegetable or meat broth
- 1 teaspoon hot sesame oil
- ¼ cup rice vinegar
- 1 cup chopped bok choy
- 1 pound (454 g) shaved steak

1. In a wok over high heat, heat the cooking oil until it shimmers.
2. Add the ginger, garlic, and carrot and Stir-fryfor 30 seconds.
3. Add the onion and mushrooms and Stir-fryfor 30 seconds.
4. Add the broth, sesame oil, and rice vinegar and bring to a boil.
5. Add the bok choy and steak and stir for 30 seconds.
6. Serve immediately.

Eggy Tofu and Sesame Soup

Prep time: 10 minutes | Cook time: 15 minutes | Serves 6

- 8 ounces / 227 g frozen Shepherd's purse
- ½ block silken tofu
- 4 cups homemade chicken stock
- 1½ teaspoon salt
- 1 teaspoon sesame oil
- ¼ teaspoon ground white pepper
- ¼ cup cornstarch, mixed with ¼ cup water
- 3 egg whites

1. Sauté tofu and shepherd's purse with sesame oil to a wok for 5 minutes.
2. Stir in stock, salt, and white pepper to taste, then cook this mixture on a simmer for 10 minutes.
3. Mix cornstarch with water and pour into the soup.
4. Cook the soup until it thickens.
5. Beat egg whites and pour into the soup.
6. Cook for 5 minutes, then serve warm.

Stir-Fried Vegetable with Brothy Soup

Prep time: 10 minutes | Cook time: 8 minutes | Serves 4

- 2 tablespoons cooking oil
- 2 garlic cloves, crushed and chopped
- 1 tablespoon crushed, chopped ginger
- 1 pound (454 g) tofu, well drained, patted dry, and cut into 1-inch pieces
- 1 red bell pepper, cut into ¼-inch pieces
- 4 ounces (113 g) mushrooms, cut into slices
- 1 cup chopped bok choy
- 1 teaspoon hot sesame oil
- 2 quarts vegetable or meat broth
- 4 eggs, beaten

1. In a wok over high heat, heat the cooking oil until it shimmers.
2. Add the garlic, ginger, and tofu and Stir-fryuntil the tofu begins to brown.
3. Add the bell pepper and Stir-fryfor 1 minute.
4. Add the mushrooms and Stir-fryfor 30 seconds.
5. Add the bok choy and Stir-fryfor 30 seconds.
6. Add the sesame oil, then add the broth and bring to a boil.
7. Drizzle the beaten eggs over the broth and let the eggs float to the top. Serve the soup hot as an appetizer or main dish.

Spicy Egg Drop Soup

Prep time: 10 minutes | Cook time: 11 minutes | Serves 4

- 2 tablespoons oil
- 10 ounces (283 g) tomatoes; cut into chunks
- 1 cup chicken stock
- 2 cups water
- 2 teaspoons light soy sauce
- ½ teaspoon sesame oil
- ¼ teaspoon white pepper
- Salt, to taste
- 1 egg, beaten
- 1½ teaspoons cornstarch mixed with 2 tablespoons water
- 1 scallion, chopped
- 2 tablespoons cilantro, chopped

1. Sauté tomatoes with oil in a deep wok for 5 minutes.
2. Stir in stock, water, soy sauce, sesame oil, white pepper, and salt, then cook for 5 minutes.
3. Pour in cornstarch slurry then cook until the soup thickens.
4. Stir in egg and cook for 1 minute.
5. Garnish with scallion and cilantro.
6. Enjoy.

Egg Meatballs with Melon Soup

Prep time: 15 minutes | Cook time: 2 minutes | Serves 6

FOR THE MEATBALLS:

- 1 pound (454 g) ground pork
- 2 tablespoons water
- 2½ tablespoons light soy sauce
- 2 tablespoons Shaoxing wine
- 1 teaspoon sesame oil
- ½ teaspoon ground white pepper
- ½ teaspoon sugar
- 1 egg white
- 1 tablespoon ginger, minced
- 1 scallion, chopped
- ¼ teaspoon salt
- For the Soup:
- 1 package glass noodles, boiled
- 1 pound (454 g) winter melon, peeled and diced
- 1 tablespoon oil
- 2 scallions, chopped
- 4 cups chicken stock
- 2 cups water
- ½ teaspoon ground white pepper
- ½ teaspoon sesame oil
- Salt, to taste
- 1 handful of cilantros, chopped

1. Mix pork with water, soy sauce, wine, sesame oil, white pepper, sugar, egg white, ginger, scallions, and salt in a bowl.
2. Make small meatballs out of this pork mixture.
3. Sauté meatballs with 1 tablespoon oil in a deep wok until golden-brown.
4. Stir in scallions and melon then sauté for 2 minutes.
5. Add the remaining soup along with boiled noodles.
6. Cook the soup for 10 minutes on medium heat until meatballs are done.
7. Serve warm.

Carrots with Pork Soup

Prep time: 10 minutes | Cook time: 3 hours | Serves 14

- 4 dried shiitake mushrooms, soaked and drained
- 1⅓ pounds (605 g) lean pork shoulder,
- 1 pound (454 g) large carrots, cut into chunks
- 2 tablespoons dried red dates, pitted and halved
- 2 tablespoons dried goji berries
- 1 large chunk ginger, smashed
- 14 cups water
- 1 pound (454 g) Chinese yams, peeled and cut into chunks
- Salt, to taste

1. Add pork, mushrooms, carrots, red dates, goji berries, ginger, water, and salt to a wok.
2. Cover and cook for 2 hours on a simmer, then add Chinese yam.
3. Cook for another 1 hour on a simmer.
4. Serve warm.

Goji Berries with Pork Ribs Soup

Prep time: 10 minutes | Cook time: 4 hours | Serves 6 to 8

- 1 pound (454 g) pork ribs, cut into 1-inch pieces
- 1 pound (454 g) lotus root, peeled and cut into ¼-inch-thick rounds
- ½ teaspoon peppercorns
- 12 cups water
- 2 tablespoons soy sauce
- 1 teaspoon salt
- ¼ cup dried goji berries
- ½ cup dried red dates (optional)

1. Place the pork ribs, lotus root, peppercorns, red dates (if using), and water in a wok.
2. Simmer over low heat for at least 4 hours, and up to 6 hours.
3. Turn off the heat and add the soy sauce, salt, and goji berries.
4. Allow the soup to sit for about 15 minutes for the goji berries to reconstitute, then serve.

Milky Laksa Noodle Soup

Prep time: 15 minutes | Cook time: 11 minutes | Serves 6

- 4 bone-in chicken thighs
- 4 tablespoons vegetable oil
- 1 garlic clove, minced
- 1½ tablespoons ginger, minced
- 1 stalk lemongrass, minced
- 2 Thai chilies, minced
- 1 tablespoon brown sugar
- 4 cups chicken stock
- 1 can coconut milk
- 1 tablespoon fish sauce
- 1 package soy puffs, halved
- 4 portions noodles
- 1 to 3 limes, juices
- 3 large shallots, thinly sliced
- ¼ cup all-purpose flour
- 12 large shrimp
- 2 cups mung bean sprouts
- ½ cup fresh cilantro leaves

1. Season the chicken thighs with black pepper and salt.
2. Place them in a baking tray and bake for 40 minutes at 400°F (205°C).
3. Meanwhile, sauté ginger and garlic with 2 tablespoons oil for 1 minute in a deep wok.
4. Stir in chilies and lemongrass then sauté for 3 minutes.
5. Add brown sugar and laksa paste, then cook for 3 minutes.
6. Stir in fish sauce, coconut milk, and chicken stock, then cook this mixture to a boil.
7. Add soy puffs, cover the soup, and cook for 10 minutes on a simmer.
8. Cook the noodles in boiling water according to the package's instructions.
9. Add noodles along with remaining to the soup.
10. Cook for 5 minutes, then serve warm.

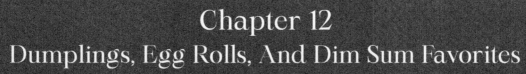

Chapter 12
Dumplings, Egg Rolls, And Dim Sum Favorites

Scallion Pancakes

Prep time: 5 minutes | Cook time: 45 minutes| Serves 4

- 2 cups all-purpose flour, plus additional for dusting
- ¾ cup warm water
- ½ cup cold water
- 2 to 4 tablespoons vegetable or peanut oil, plus additional as needed
- 3 or 4 scallions, thinly sliced

1. In a large bowl, mix the flour and warm water together to form a dough. Work the cold water into the dough, a little bit at a time, until a smooth and not too sticky dough forms.
2. On a clean work surface, knead the dough for 10 minutes. If the dough seems too sticky at first, dust the work surface with a little flour. The dough will become smoother the more it is kneaded, and extra flour should not be necessary. Place the dough back in the bowl, and cover it with a damp cloth or paper towel. Let the dough rest for 30 minutes.
3. Roll each piece of dough into a level circle, 7 to 8 inches in diameter. Brush the top of each circle lightly with some of the oil. Top each circle with one quarter of the scallions.
4. Fold the edges of the dough over the top of the scallions to create a ball. Then flatten the dough and roll out each again to incorporate the scallions into the dough.
5. Heat your wok over medium-low heat. Using about ½ to 1 tablespoon of oil, lightly fry each dough circle until golden brown, 2 to 3 minutes per side.
6. Serve warm with Sesame Dipping Sauce or regular soy sauce.

Perfect Pork Pot Stickers

Prep time: 35 minutes | Cook time: 10 minutes| Serves 4 as an appetizer

- 12 ounces napa cabbage leaves, chopped
- 1 teaspoon kosher salt
- 1 teaspoon grated fresh ginger
- ¼ cup minced scallions
- 1 pound ground pork
- ⅛ teaspoon white pepper
- 1½ tablespoons soy sauce
- 1 tablespoon Shaoxing rice wine
- 2 teaspoons toasted sesame oil
- 30 to 40 dumpling wrappers (gyoza, pot sticker, or mandu)
- 1½ tablespoons peanut or vegetable oil
- ¼ cup water, room temperature or warm

1. Put the cabbage in a strainer in the sink or over a bowl, and sprinkle it with the kosher salt. Mix the kosher salt with the cabbage to coat the cabbage. Let the cabbage sit for 15 minutes. Using your hands, squeeze any water from the cabbage, getting as much out as possible.
2. In a medium bowl, mix together the cabbage, ginger, scallions, pork, white pepper, soy sauce, rice wine, and sesame oil. Using your hands, mix the ingredients thoroughly until they are sticky.
3. Heat a wok to medium-high, and add the peanut oil. Place the pot stickers into the wok, seam-side up. Cook the dumplings for about 1 minute, until the bottoms are golden brown.
4. Remove the wok from the heat.
5. Serve warm with your favorite hot chili sauce or dumpling dipping sauce.

HOW TO
Fold a Pot Sticker or Dumpling

1 .... Hold the wrapper in one hand and place 1 tablespoon of filling in the center of the wrapper. Wet your finger and trace the entire edge of the wrapper to dampen it.

2 .... Gently fold the wrapper in half, but do not seal the edges together.

3 .... Use your right thumb and index finger to make a small pleat in the top layer of the wrapper, leaving the bottom layer un-pleated. Press the pleated layer together with the un-pleated layer. Repeat 5 to 6 times.

4..Run your fingers along the edges of the wrapper together to ensure that the pot sticker or dumpling is completely sealed.

Easy Egg and Scallion Dumplings
Prep time: 5 minutes | Cook time: 15 minutes| Serves 4

- 2 tablespoons vegetable or peanut oil
- ½ teaspoon toasted sesame oil
- 1 teaspoon minced garlic
- 4 large eggs, beaten
- Sea salt
- Freshly ground black pepper
- 2 scallions, trimmed and chopped
- 24 to 30 dumpling, gyoza, or pot sticker wrappers

1. To a hot wok, add the vegetable oil and sesame oil. Add the garlic and cook for about 30 seconds.
2. Add the eggs to the wok, and season with the sea salt and pepper. Scramble the eggs with a heat-proof spatula for about 30 seconds, or until done. Add the scallions and mix with the scrambled eggs. Transfer the eggs to a plate, and set aside to cool until they can be handled.
3. Spoon a heaping teaspoon of the egg and scallion filling into the center of a dumpling wrapper. Wet the edges of the wrapper with water, fold the wrapper to enclose the filling, and seal the dumpling by pinching the wrapper at its edges. Repeat with the remaining wrappers and filling. Make sure the un-cooked dumplings don't touch each other. They will stick together until they're cooked.
4. Steam, pan-fry, boil, or deep-fry the dumplings, or use them in soup.

HOW TO
Fold an Egg Roll

1 .... Place the wrapper on a clean surface with one point facing you. Spread 1 tablespoon of the filling on the wrapper in a horizontal line slightly closer to you.

2 .... Roll the point of the wrapper closer to you over the filling.

3 .... Fold in the two side corners of the wrapper.

4 .... Dampen the remaining open point of the wrapper with water. Finish rolling the egg roll away from you.

Vegetable Egg Rolls

Prep time: 5 minutes | Cook time: 25 minutes | Serves 4

- 2 tablespoons plus 1 teaspoon peanut oil, divided
- 2 garlic cloves, minced
- 1 tablespoon minced fresh ginger or ⅓ teaspoon ground ginger
- ½ sweet onion, thinly sliced
- 1 celery stalk, thinly sliced
- 2 carrots, cut into matchsticks
- ½ small cabbage, shredded
- 2 tablespoons rice vinegar
- 2 teaspoons soy sauce
- 1 teaspoon sugar
- 40 to 50 egg roll wrappers

1. To a hot wok over medium-high heat, add 1 teaspoon of peanut oil, the garlic, and the ginger, and Stir-fry for about 30 seconds. Add the onion, celery, and carrots to the wok, and Stir-fry for about 2 minutes. Add the cabbage, rice vinegar, soy sauce, and sugar. Stir-fry the mixture for another 2 minutes. Remove the vegetables from the wok, and let them cool until they can be handled.
2. Place the egg roll wrappers on a clean surface with a point facing you. Spread 1 tablespoon of the filling in a horizontal line, slightly closer to you. Roll the point of the wrapper closest to you over the filling. Fold in the two side corners. Dampen the remaining open point with water, and finish rolling the egg roll away from you.
3. The egg rolls will be fried in two batches. To a wok over medium-high heat, add 1 tablespoon of the peanut oil. Place the egg rolls in the wok, seam-side down. Fry them for about 5 to 8 minutes, turning often so they cook evenly. Repeat this step with the rest of the egg rolls.
4. Serve with plum sauce, sweet and sour sauce, chili sauce, or duck sauce.

HOW TO
Fold a Wonton

1 .... Place the wonton wrapper on a clean surface with the point facing you. In the center of the wonton wrapper, place 1 teaspoon of the filling.

2 .... Dampen the edges of the wonton wrapper with water. Fold over the edges of the wrapper to make a triangle. Ensure that the edges are sealed.

3 .... Pull in the two side points of the triangle together so that one overlaps the other. Press them together to ensure that they are sealed.

Quick-Fried Wontons at Home
Prep time: 5 minutes | Cook time: 35 minutes| Serves 4

- 1 pound ground pork
- 2 garlic cloves, minced
- 1 teaspoon minced fresh ginger
- 1 teaspoon toasted sesame oil
- 1 tablespoon soy sauce
- 5 scallions, finely chopped
- 2 carrots, finely chopped
- 40 to 50 wonton wrappers
- Peanut oil, for deep-frying

1. In a large bowl, mix together the pork, garlic, ginger, sesame oil, soy sauce, scallions, and carrots.
2. In the center of a wonton wrapper, place about a teaspoon of the pork filling. Dampen the edges of the wonton wrapper with a little water, and fold the edges over to make a triangle. Using your fingers, press the edges together to seal the wonton.
3. To a wok, add enough of the peanut oil so that it is about 1½ inches deep. Heat the oil to 350°F. Fry 5 or 6 wontons at a time until they're golden brown. Continue until all are fried.
4. Drain the finished wontons on a rack or a plate covered with paper towels. Serve with chili sauce or sweet and sour sauce.

Simple Shanghai Buns
Prep time: 5 minutes | Cook time: 45 minutes| Serves 4

- 2 cups all-purpose flour
- 2 teaspoons yeast
- 2 teaspoons baking powder
- 2 teaspoons sugar
- ½ cup chopped napa cabbage
- 1½ pounds lean ground beef
- 2 tablespoons soy sauce
- 1 teaspoon toasted sesame oil
- Black vinegar (for dipping)

1. To make the dough, mix together the flour, yeast, baking powder, and sugar in a medium mixing bowl. Let the dough rest for 30 minutes.
2. In a large bowl, mix the cabbage, ground beef, soy sauce, and sesame oil together.
3. Once the dough has rested, divide it into 15 equal pieces. Roll a dough piece into a circle, about 4 inches in diameter. Put about 1 tablespoon of filling in the center of the dough circle. Bring the edges of the dough together at the top, and twist and pinch them together to seal. Repeat this for the remaining dough pieces and the filling.
4. Add about 2 inches of water to your wok. Place a piece of parchment paper in the bottom of a bamboo steamer, and put the steamer in the wok. Bring the water to a boil.
5. Place the buns in the bamboo steamer, making sure they do not touch. Cover the steamer and steam the buns until they are cooked, about 15 minutes.

6. Serve with black vinegar or your favorite dumpling dipping sauce on the side.

Pork Shumai
Prep time: 5 minutes | Cook time: 50 minutes| Serves 4

- For the dipping sauce
- 3 tablespoons soy sauce
- 1 tablespoon chili sauce
- 1 teaspoon sesame oil

FOR THE FILLING
- 2 tablespoons soy sauce
- 2 tablespoons sherry wine
- 1½ teaspoons sesame oil
- 2 teaspoons sugar
- ½ teaspoon salt
- 1½ teaspoons grated fresh ginger
- 4 scallions, chopped
- 3 garlic cloves, minced
- 2 shiitake mushrooms, chopped
- Freshly ground black pepper
- 1 pound ground pork
- 30 to 40 wonton wrappers

1. To a large bowl, add the soy sauce, sherry wine, sesame oil, sugar, salt, ginger, scallions, garlic, and mushrooms. Season with the pepper and mix well. Add the pork to the bowl, and mix to combine well.
2. Place 2 tablespoons of filling in the center of a wonton wrapper. Using your fingers, wet the edges of the wrapper with some water. Gather the sides of the wrapper together so that the wrapper pleats, leaving the top open. Gently flatten the bottom so the shumai can sit upright. Repeat this step with the rest of the wonton wrappers until all the filling is gone. Refrigerate the shumai for about 30 minutes. Leave enough space between each shumai so they do not touch each other or they will stick together.
3. Add 1½ cups of water to your wok. Place a piece of parchment paper in the bottom of a bamboo steamer and put the steamer in the wok. Bring the water to a boil.
4. Place the shumai in the bamboo steamer, making sure they do not touch. Cover the steamer and steam the shumai 8 to 10 minutes, until they are cooked.
5. Serve with chili-soy dipping sauce.

Crab Rangoon

Prep time: 5 minutes | Cook time: 25 minutes| Serves 4

- ½ pound cooked crabmeat or imitation crab, lightly flaked
- 5 ounces cream cheese (at room temperature)
- ½ teaspoon steak sauce
- ½ teaspoon garlic powder or 2 garlic cloves, minced
- 25 wonton wrappers
- 3 cups peanut or vegetable oil

1. To a medium bowl, add the crabmeat, cream cheese, steak sauce, and garlic powder. Mix well.
2. Place about 1 teaspoon of the filling in the center of a wonton wrapper. Moisten the edges of the wrapper with a little water. Fold the wrapper to form a triangle. Take the two outside points of the wrapper, and press them together firmly.
3. Heat the peanut oil in a wok to 375°F. Deep-fry the wontons, a few at a time, until lightly browned, about 2 minutes. Drain the finished wontons on a wire rack or paper towel–lined plate. Serve warm.

Vegetable Dumplings

Prep time: 15 minutes | Cook time: 32 minutes| Serves 12

- 12 Dumpling wrappers

FILLING

- 3 tablespoons oil
- 1 tablespoon ginger, minced
- 1 large onion, chopped
- 2 cups shiitake mushrooms, chopped
- 1½ cups cabbage, shredded
- 1½ cups carrot, shredded
- 1 cup garlic chives, chopped
- ½ teaspoon white pepper
- 2 teaspoons sesame oil
- 3 tablespoons Shaoxing wine
- 2 tablespoon soy sauce
- 1 teaspoon sugar
- Salt, to taste

1. Sauté onion with oil in a Mandarin wok until soft.
2. Stir in ginger, mushrooms, cabbage, garlic, and rest of the ingredients.
3. Sauté for about 7–10 minutes until veggies are cooked and soft.
4. Allow the filling to cool and spread the dumpling wrappers on the working surface.
5. Divide the mushroom filling at the center of each dumpling wrapper.
6. Wet the edges of the dumplings and bring all the edges of each dumpling together.
7. Pinch and seal the edges of the dumplings to seal the filling inside.
8. Boil water in a suitable pot with a steamer basket placed inside.
9. Add the dumplings to the steamer, cover and

steam for 20 minutes.
10. Meanwhile, heat about 2 tablespoons oil in a Mandarin wok.
11. Sear the dumpling for 2 minutes until golden.
12. Serve warm.

Shrimp Dumplings

Prep time: 5 minutes | Cook time: 8 minutes| Serves 4

- ½ pound raw shrimp, peeled, deveined
- 1 teaspoon oyster sauce
- 1 tablespoon vegetable oil
- ¼ teaspoon white pepper
- 1 teaspoon sesame oil
- ¼ teaspoon salt
- 1 teaspoon sugar
- ½ teaspoon ginger, minced
- ¼ cup bamboo shoots, chopped
- 12 dumpling wrappers

1. Blend shrimp with all the filling Prep time: 5 minutes | Cook time: 15 minutes| Serves 4(except bamboo shoots) in a blender.
2. Add bamboo shoots to the blended filling and mix well.
3. Cover and refrigerate this filling for 1 hour.
4. Meanwhile, spread the dumpling wrappers on the working surface.
5. Divide the shrimp filling at the center of each dumpling wrapper.
6. Wet the edges of the dumplings and bring all the edges of each dumpling together.
7. Pinch and seal the edges of the dumplings to seal the filling inside.
8. Boil water in a suitable pot with a steamer basket placed inside.
9. Add the dumplings to the steamer, cover and steam for 6 minutes.
10. Meanwhile, heat about 2 tablespoons oil in a Mandarin wok.
11. Sear the dumpling for 2 minutes until golden.
12. Serve warm.

Buffalo Chicken Pot Stickers

Prep time: 5 minutes | Cook time: 25 minutes| Serves 24

- 4 tablespoons oil
- 1 medium onion, finely chopped
- 2 stalks celery, chopped
- 1 pound ground chicken
- ½ cup Frank's hot sauce
- 2 cups cheddar cheese, shredded
- Salt and black pepper, to taste
- 48 dumpling wrappers

1. Sauté onion and celery with oil in a Mandarin wok until soft.
2. Stir in chicken and cook until it is golden-brown.
3. Add hot sauce, cheddar cheese, black pepper, and salt.
4. Mix well and cook this filling for 5 minutes.
5. Allow the filling to cool and spread the dumpling wrappers on the working surface.
6. Divide the chicken filling at the center of each dumpling wrapper.
7. Wet the edges of the dumplings and bring all the edges of each dumpling together.
8. Pinch and seal the edges of the dumplings to seal the filling inside.
9. Boil water in a suitable pot with a steamer basket placed inside.
10. Add the dumplings to the steamer, cover and steam for 8 minutes.
11. Meanwhile, heat about 2 tablespoons oil in a skillet.
12. Sear the dumpling for 2 minutes until golden.
13. Serve warm.

Chicken Mushrooms Dumplings

Prep time: 5 minutes | Cook time: 25 minutes| Serves 24

- 48 dumpling wrappers
- 2 tablespoons vegetable oil
- 1 small onion, finely chopped
- 4 ounces shiitake mushrooms, chopped
- 6 dried shiitake mushrooms, chopped
- 1 pound ground chicken
- 2 teaspoons sesame oil
- 3 tablespoons soy sauce
- 1 teaspoon sugar
- 2 tablespoons Shaoxing wine

1. Sauté onion with oil in a Mandarin wok until soft.
2. Stir in mushrooms, chicken, and rest of the ingredients.
3. Sauté for about 7 minutes until veggies are cooked and soft.
4. Allow the filling to cool and spread the dumpling wrappers on the working surface.
5. Divide the chicken filling at the center of each dumpling wrapper.
6. Wet the edges of the dumplings and bring all the edges of each dumpling together.
7. Pinch and seal the edges of the dumplings to seal

the filling inside.
8. Boil water in a suitable pot with a steamer basket placed inside.
9. Add the dumplings to the steamer, cover and steam for 10 minutes.
10. Meanwhile, heat about 2 tablespoons oil in a skillet.
11. Sear the dumpling for 2 minutes until golden.
12. Serve warm.

Eggy Scallion Dumplings

Prep time: 10 minutes | Cook time: 15 minutes | Serves 4

- 2 tablespoons vegetable or peanut oil
- ½ teaspoon toasted sesame oil
- 1 teaspoon minced garlic
- 4 large eggs, beaten
- Sea salt to taste
- Freshly ground black pepper to taste
- 2 scallions, trimmed and chopped
- 24 to 30 dumpling, gyoza, or pot sticker wrappers

1. To a hot wok, add the vegetable oil and sesame oil. Add the garlic and cook for about 30 seconds.
2. Add the eggs to the wok, and season with the sea salt and pepper to taste. Scramble the eggs with a heat-proof spatula for about 30 seconds, or until done. Add the scallions and mix with the scrambled eggs. Transfer the eggs to a plate, and set aside to cool until they can be handled.
3. Spoon a heaping teaspoon of the egg and scallion filling into the center of a dumpling wrapper. Wet the edges of the wrapper with water, fold the wrapper to enclose the filling, and seal the dumpling by pinching the wrapper at its edges. Repeat with the remaining wrappers and filling. Make sure the uncooked dumplings don't touch each other. They will stick together until they're cooked.
4. Steam, pan-fry, boil, or deep-fry the dumplings, or use them in soup.

Pepper and Ginger Shrimp Dumplings

Prep time: 10 minutes | Cook time: 8 minutes | Serves 4

- ½ pound (227g) raw shrimp, peeled, deveined
- 1 teaspoon oyster sauce
- 1 tablespoon vegetable oil
- ¼ teaspoon white pepper
- 1 teaspoon sesame oil
- ¼ teaspoon salt
- 1 teaspoon sugar
- ½ teaspoon ginger, minced
- ¼ cup bamboo shoots, chopped
- 12 dumpling wrappers

1. Blend shrimp with all the filling ingredients (except bamboo shoots) in a blender. Add bamboo shoots to the blended filling and mix well. Cover and refrigerate this filling for 1 hour.
2. Meanwhile, spread the dumpling wrappers on the working surface. Divide the shrimp filling at the center of each dumpling wrapper. Wet the edges of the dumplings and bring all the edges of each dumpling together. Pinch and seal the edges of the dumplings to seal the filling inside.
3. Boil water in a suitable pot with a steamer basket placed inside.
4. Add the dumplings to the steamer, cover and steam for 6 minutes.
5. Meanwhile, heat about 2 tablespoons oil in a Mandarin wok.
6. Sear the dumpling for 2 minutes until golden.
7. Serve warm.

Japanese Gyoza Dumplings

Prep time: 5 minutes | Cook time:30 minutes| Serves 12

- 5 cups Napa cabbage
- 8 ounces ground pork
- 1 garlic clove, smashed
- 1 ½ teaspoon fresh ginger, minced
- 1 scallion, chopped
- 2 tablespoons vegetable oil
- ½ teaspoon sesame oil
- 2 teaspoons soy sauce
- ¾ teaspoon sugar
- ½ teaspoon salt
- 1/8 teaspoons white pepper
- 24 store-bought gyoza wrappers

1. Sauté garlic, ginger, and scallions with oil in a Mandarin wok until soft.
2. Stir in cabbage, pork, and rest of the ingredients.
3. Sauté for about 7 minutes until veggies are cooked and soft.
4. Allow the filling to cool and spread the gyoza wrappers on the working surface.
5. Divide the pork filling at the center of each gyoza wrapper.
6. Wet the edges of the dumplings and bring all the edges of each wrapper together.
7. Pinch and seal the edges of the dumplings to seal the filling inside.
8. Boil water in a suitable pot with a steamer basket placed inside.
9. Add the dumplings to the steamer, cover and steam for 20 minutes.
10. Meanwhile, heat about 2 tablespoons oil in a skillet.
11. Sear the dumpling for 2 minutes until golden.
12. Serve warm.

Chicken Zucchini Dumplings

Prep time: 5 minutes | Cook time: 30 minutes| Serves 12

- 1 medium zucchini, shredded
- 2 ½ tablespoons vegetable oil
- 1 tablespoon ginger, minced
- ½ pound ground chicken
- ¼ teaspoon white pepper
- ½ teaspoon sugar
- 1 teaspoon sesame oil
- 1 ½ tablespoons soy sauce
- 1 tablespoon Shaoxing wine
- 1 package dumpling wrappers

1. Sauté ginger and zucchini with oil in a Cantonese wok until soft.
2. Stir in chicken, soy sauce, and rest of the ingredients.
3. Sauté for about 5 minutes until chicken are cooked and golden.
4. Allow the filling to cool and spread the dumpling wrappers on the working surface.
5. Divide the chicken filling at the center of each dumpling wrapper.
6. Wet the edges of the dumplings and bring all the edges of each wrapper together.
7. Pinch and seal the edges of the dumplings to seal the filling inside.
8. Boil water in a suitable pot with a steamer basket placed inside.
9. Add the dumplings to the steamer, cover and steam for 20 minutes.
10. Meanwhile, heat about 2 tablespoons oil in a skillet.
11. Sear the dumpling for 2 minutes until golden.
12. Serve warm.

Fried Spring Rolls
Prep time: 5 minutes | Cook time: 60 minutes| Serves 10

- 1 2/3 ounces dried mung bean noodles
- 1 pound ground pork
- 2 medium carrots, grated
- 1/3 cup rehydrated wood ear mushrooms, chopped
- ¼ cup shallots, chopped
- 1 garlic clove, minced
- 1 teaspoon ginger, grated
- 1 egg white
- 1 tablespoon fish sauce
- 1 tablespoon vegetable oil
- ½ teaspoon salt
- ¼ teaspoon ground white pepper
- 1 cup warm water
- 20 dried rice paper wrappers
- Canola or vegetable oil, for frying

1. Soak the noodles in boiling water for 30 minutes, then drain.
2. Sauté carrots, shallots, and mushrooms with oil in a Mandarin wok until soft.
3. Stir in pork and rest of the ingredients.
4. Sauté for about 7 minutes until veggies are cooked and soft.
5. Allow the filling to cool and spread the rice paper wrappers on the working surface.
6. Divide the pork filling at the center of each wrapper.
7. Wet the edges of the dumplings and bring all the edges of each wrapper together.
8. Pinch and seal the edges of the dumplings to seal the filling inside.
9. Boil water in a suitable pot with a steamer basket placed inside.
10. Add the dumplings to the steamer, cover and steam for 20 minutes.
11. Meanwhile, heat about 2 tablespoons oil in a skillet.
12. Sear the dumpling for 2 minutes until golden.
13. Serve warm.

Egg Rolls
Prep time: 5 minutes | Cook time: 27 minutes| Serves 12

- 8 cups savoy cabbage, shredded
- 8 cups green cabbage, shredded
- 2 cups carrot, shredded
- 2 cups celery, shredded
- 3 scallions, chopped
- 2 ½ teaspoon salt
- 2 teaspoons sugar
- 1 tablespoon sesame oil
- 2 tablespoons peanut oil
- ¼ teaspoon five-spice powder
- ¼ teaspoon white pepper
- 3 cups roast pork minced
- 2 cups cooked shrimp, chopped
- 1 package egg roll wrappers

1. Sauté scallions, cabbage, carrot, and celery with oil in a Mandarin wok until soft.
2. Stir in pork, shrimp, and rest of the ingredients.
3. Sauté for about 7 minutes until chicken are cooked and golden.
4. Allow the filling to cool and spread the egg roll wrappers on the working surface.
5. Divide the pork filling at the center of each wrapper.
6. Wet the edges of the wrapper, fold the two sides then roll the wrappers into an egg roll.
7. Add oil to a deep wok to 325°F then deep fry the egg rolls until golden-brown.
8. Transfer the golden egg rolls to a plate lined with paper towel.
9. Serve warm.

Shanghai-Style Spring Rolls
Prep time: 5 minutes | Cook time: 25 minutes| Serves 8

- 2/3 cup lean pork, shredded
- 1 small Napa cabbage, shredded
- 8 dried shiitake mushrooms, soaked
- 4 tablespoons oil
- Salt, to taste
- White pepper, to taste
- 2 tablespoons Shaoxing wine
- ½ teaspoon soy sauce
- 1 ½ tablespoon cornstarch, mixed with one tablespoon water
- 2 teaspoons sesame oil
- 24 roll wrappers
- Oil, for frying

1. Mix pork, cabbage, mushrooms, with rest of the ingredients in a bowl (except the roll wrappers).
2. Sauté the filling in a Cantonese wok for about 10 minutes.
3. Allow the filling to cool and spread the egg roll wrappers on the working surface.
4. Divide the pork filling at the center of each wrapper.
5. Wet the edges of the wrapper, fold the two sides, then roll the wrappers into an egg roll.
6. Add oil to a deep wok to 325°F then deep fry the egg rolls until golden-brown.
7. Transfer the golden egg rolls to a plate lined with paper towel.
8. Serve warm.

Chicken Phyllo Rolls
Prep time: 5 minutes | Cook time: 15 minutes| Serves 12

- 2 tablespoons olive oil
- 1 small onion, sliced
- 2 scallions, chopped
- 3 garlic cloves, minced
- 2 teaspoons curry powder
- 2 cups cooked chicken, shredded
- 1 tablespoon cilantro, chopped
- 1 lime, zested
- 2 tablespoons lime juice
- Salt, to taste
- Black pepper, to taste
- 4 tablespoons butter, melted
- 8 sheets phyllo dough
- ¼ cup panko breadcrumbs

1. Sauté onion, scallions, and garlic with oil in a Mandarin wok until soft.
2. Stir in chicken and rest of the ingredients(except the phyllo dough).
3. Sauté for about 1 minute then remove the filling from the heat.
4. Spread a sheet of dough phyllo in a baking pan and brush it with butter.
5. Drizzle breadcrumbs on top, repeat the layers with three more phyllo sheets.
6. Top the four phyllo sheets with ½ of the chicken filling.
7. Roll the sheets to make a phyllo roll.
8. Repeat the same steps with remaining phyllo and filling.
9. Place the rolls in a baking tray and brush them with butter.
10. Bake the phyllo rolls for 12 minutes in the oven at 375°F.
11. Slice and serve warm.

Cream Cheese Wontons
Prep time: 5 minutes | Cook time: 25 minutes| Serves 6

- 8 ounces cream cheese
- 2 teaspoons sugar
- ½ teaspoon salt
- 4 scallions, chopped
- 1 pack wonton wrappers
- Vegetable oil, for frying

HOW TO PREPARE
1. Mix cream cheese with sugar, salt, and scallions in a bowl.
2. Spread the egg roll wrappers on the working surface.
3. Divide the cream cheese filling at the center of each wrapper.
4. Wet the edges of the wrapper, fold the two sides, then roll the wrappers into an egg roll.
5. Add oil to a deep wok to 325°F then deep fry the egg rolls until golden-brown.
6. Transfer the golden egg rolls to a plate lined with a paper towel.
7. Serve warm.

San Xian Wontons
Prep time: 5 minutes | Cook time: 25 minutes| Serves 12

- 8 ounces shrimp; peeled, deveined, and chopped
- 8 ounces ground pork
- 8 ounces ground chicken
- 1 tablespoon ginger, minced
- ¼ cup scallion, chopped
- 2 tablespoons vegetable oil
- 2 tablespoons light soy sauce
- 1 tablespoon oyster sauce
- ½ tablespoon sesame oil
- ½ teaspoon ground white pepper
- ½ cup water
- 2 packages wonton wrappers

1. Sauté scallions and ginger with oil in a Mandarin wok until soft.
2. Stir in pork, chicken, shrimp, and rest of the ingredients(except the wrappers).
3. Sauté for about 8 minutes, then remove the filling from the heat.
4. Allow the filling to cool and spread the egg roll wrappers on the working surface.
5. Divide the pork-shrimp filling at the center of each wrapper.
6. Wet the edges of the wrapper, fold the two sides then roll the wrappers into an egg roll.
7. Add oil to a deep wok to 325°F then deep fry the egg rolls until golden-brown.
8. Transfer the golden egg rolls to a plate lined with a paper towel.
9. Serve warm.

Mushroom with Cilantro Garbanzo
Prep time: 10 minutes | Cook time: 25 minutes | Serves 2

- 2 tablespoons oil
- 1 tablespoon. oregano
- 1 tablespoon. chopped basil
- 1 clove garlic, crushed
- ground black pepper to taste
- 2 cups cooked garbanzo beans
- 1 large zucchini, halved and sliced
- ½ cup sliced mushrooms
- 1 tablespoon. chopped cilantro
- 1 tomato, chopped

1. Heat oil in a skillet over medium heat. Stir in oregano, basil, garlic and pepper. Add the garbanzo beans and zucchini, stirring well to coat with oil and herbs. Cook for 10 minutes, stirring occasionally.
2. Stir in mushrooms and cilantro; cook 10 minutes, stirring occasionally. Place the chopped tomato on top of the mixture to steam. Cover and cook 5 minutes more.

Carrot with Chicken Salad Cups
Prep time: 15 minutes | Cook time: 8 minutes | Makes 15 to 20

FOR THE CHICKEN CUPS:

- 4 ounces (113 g) skinless, boneless chicken tenderloins
- Salt and Pepper to taste
- 3 tablespoons olive oil, divided
- 15 to 20 wonton wrappers
- 1 small head romaine lettuce, shredded
- 1 carrot, julienned
- 2 scallions, chopped
- ¼ cup sliced almonds
- ¼ cup chopped fresh cilantro
- For the salad dressing:
- 4 tablespoons apple cider vinegar
- 2 tablespoons sesame oil
- 2 tablespoons honey

1. Season the chicken tenderloins with salt and pepper to taste. In a wok over medium heat, heat 1 tablespoon of olive oil. Add the chicken and sear on both sides until cooked through, about 1 minute per side. Remove the chicken from the wok and chop it finely.
2. Preheat the oven to 375°F (190°C).
3. Brush each wonton wrapper on both sides with a thin layer of olive oil. Arrange the wonton wrappers in a regular-size muffin pan to form little cups.
4. Bake the wrappers for 6 minutes. Allow them to cool completely.
5. While the wrappers are baking, make the salad dressing. Combine the apple cider vinegar, sesame oil, and honey in a small bowl, and mix well.
6. In a large bowl, combine the chicken, lettuce, carrot, scallions, almonds, and cilantro with the salad dressing and toss well.
7. Fill each wonton cup with the salad and serve.

Spicy Shrimp with Pork Shumai
Prep time: 15 minutes | Cook time: 10 minutes | Makes 20 to 25

- ½ pound (227g) shrimp, peeled and deveined
- ½ pound (227g) ground pork
- 3 tablespoons sesame oil
- 1 tablespoon cornstarch
- 1 tablespoon soy sauce
- 1 teaspoon grated ginger
- ½ teaspoon salt
- 2 pinches ground white pepper
- 2 teaspoons Shaoxing wine
- 20 to 25 round wonton wrappers
- ½ carrot, finely minced

1. Mince the shrimp by flattening each piece with the side of a knife, then roughly chopping each one.
2. Mix together the shrimp and the ground pork.
3. Add the sesame oil, cornstarch, soy sauce, ginger, salt, pepper, and Shaoxing wine to the shrimp and pork. Combine thoroughly.
4. Make an "O" with your thumb and index finger. Place one wonton wrapper on the "O" and gently press it down to create a small cup.
5. Using a teaspoon, fill the wonton cup to the top with some of the pork and shrimp mixture. Use the back of the teaspoon to press the filling into the cup.
6. Line a bamboo steamer with parchment paper liners or napa cabbage leaves. Arrange the shumai on top of the liners or leaves. Top each shumai with a bit of minced carrot.
7. Steam for 10 minutes or until the meat is cooked through.

Scallion with Cheesy Cream Wontons
Prep time: 10 minutes | Cook time: 20 minutes | Serves 6

- 8 ounces / 227 g cream cheese
- 2 teaspoons sugar
- ½ teaspoon salt
- 4 scallions, chopped
- 1 pack wonton wrappers
- Vegetable oil, for frying

1. Mix cream cheese with sugar, salt, and scallions in a bowl. Spread the egg roll wrappers on the working surface.
2. Divide the cream cheese filling at the center of each wrapper.
3. Wet the edges of the wrapper, fold the two sides, then roll the wrappers into an egg roll.
4. Add oil to a deep wok to 325°F (163°C) then deep fry the egg rolls until golden-brown.
5. Transfer the golden egg rolls to a plate lined with a paper towel.
6. Serve warm.

Eggy Crab Lettuce Warps

Prep time: 10 minutes | Cook time: 10 minutes | Serves 4 to 6

- 1 head lettuce
- 4 eggs, lightly beaten
- Pinch salt to taste
- Pinch ground white pepper to taste
- ½ teaspoon soy sauce
- 2 scallions, chopped
- 3 tablespoons peanut oil
- ½ cup diced water chestnuts
- 1 small onion, thinly sliced
- ¾ cup crabmeat

1. Wash and separate the lettuce leaves. Chill the lettuce leaves in the refrigerator until just before serving.
2. Put the beaten eggs into a medium bowl. Add the salt, pepper, soy sauce, and scallions to the eggs. Stir gently just to combine.
3. In a wok over medium-high heat, heat the peanut oil.
4. Stir-fry the water chestnuts and onion until the onion is slightly translucent.
5. Add the crabmeat to the wok, then the egg mixture, and let it sit for a moment. When the bottom of the egg is cooked through, flip, and cook on the other side.
6. Using a wok spatula, break up and scramble the egg.
7. Serve with the chilled lettuce leaves and sambal (if using).

Limey Chicken Phyllo Rolls

Prep time: 10 minutes | Cook time: 15 minutes | Serves 12

- 2 tablespoons olive oil
- 1 small onion, sliced
- 2 scallions, chopped
- 3 garlic cloves, minced
- 2 teaspoons curry powder
- 2 cups cooked chicken, shredded
- 1 tablespoon cilantro, chopped
- 1 lime, zested
- 2 tablespoons lime juice
- Salt, to taste
- Black pepper, to taste
- 4 tablespoons butter, melted
- 8 sheets phyllo dough
- ¼ cup panko breadcrumbs

1. Sauté onion, scallions, and garlic with oil in a Mandarin wok until soft. Stir in chicken and rest of the ingredients (except the phyllo dough). Sauté for about 1 minute then remove the filling from the heat.
2. Spread a sheet of dough phyllo in a baking pan and brush it with butter. Drizzle breadcrumbs on top, repeat the layers with three more phyllo sheets.
3. Top the four phyllo sheets with ½ of the chicken filling. Roll the sheets to make a phyllo roll.
4. Repeat the same steps with remaining phyllo and filling.
5. Place the rolls in a baking tray and brush them with butter. Bake the phyllo rolls for 12 minutes in the oven at 375°F (190°C).
6. Slice and serve warm.

San Xian Wontons

Prep time: 10 minutes | Cook time: 20 minutes | Serves 12

- 8 ounces shrimp; peeled, deveined, and chopped
- 8 ounces ground pork
- 8 ounces ground chicken
- 1 tablespoon ginger, minced
- ¼ cup scallion, chopped
- 2 tablespoons vegetable oil
- 2 tablespoons light soy sauce
- 1 tablespoon oyster sauce
- ½ tablespoon sesame oil
- ½ teaspoon ground white pepper
- ½ cup water
- 2 packages wonton wrappers

1. Sauté scallions and ginger with oil in a Mandarin wok until soft.
2. Stir in pork, chicken, shrimp, and rest of the ingredients (except the wrappers).
3. Sauté for about 8 minutes, then remove the filling from the heat.
4. Allow the filling to cool and spread the egg roll wrappers on the working surface.
5. Divide the pork-shrimp filling at the center of each wrapper.
6. Wet the edges of the wrapper, fold the two sides then roll the wrappers into an egg roll.
7. Add oil to a deep wok to 325°F then deep fry the egg rolls until golden-brown.
8. Transfer the golden egg rolls to a plate lined with a paper towel.
9. Serve warm.

Vinegary Napa Cabbage Salad

Prep time: 20 minutes | Cook time: 0 minutes | Serves 4 as a side

- 1 tablespoon toasted sesame oil
- 1 tablespoon soy sauce
- 3 tablespoons rice vinegar or white vinegar
- 1 tablespoon sugar
- 3 cups finely shredded napa cabbage
- 1 cup shredded carrots
- 1 scallion, finely slivered

1. In a large bowl, whisk together the sesame oil, soy sauce, rice vinegar, and sugar. Add the cabbage, carrots, and slivered scallion. Toss to combine.

Avocado with Tofu and Scallion Salad

Prep time: 10 minutes | Cook time: 5 minutes | Serves 4

- 7 ounces (198 g) silken tofu, sliced
- 1 ripe avocado, peeled and sliced
- 2 garlic cloves, grated
- 1 teaspoon ginger, grated
- 2 tablespoons light soy sauce
- 1 teaspoon sesame oil
- ½ teaspoon sugar
- ½ teaspoon Chinese black vinegar
- ¼ teaspoon white pepper
- 2 teaspoons water
- Salt, to taste
- 1 scallion, finely chopped

1. Sauté tofu with sesame oil in a Mandarin wok for 5 minutes.
2. Toss tofu with rest of the salad ingredients in a salad bowl.
3. Mix well and serve.
4. Enjoy.

Vinegary Sesame with Cucumber Salad

Prep time: 10 minutes | Cook time: 2 minutes | Serves 4

6 garlic cloves, minced
3 tablespoons oil
2 English cucumbers, sliced
1 ½ teaspoon salt
1 teaspoon sugar
⅛ teaspoon MSG
¼ teaspoon sesame oil
1 tablespoon rice vinegar

1. Sauté garlic with oil in a Cantonese wok for 30 seconds.
2. Stir in sugar, MSG, sesame oil, rice vinegar, and salt.
3. Cook for 1 minute, then toss in cucumber.
4. Mix well and serve.

Garlicky Egg and Scallion Dumplings

Prep time: 10 minutes | Cook time: 15 minutes | Serves 4

- 2 tablespoons vegetable or peanut oil
- ½ teaspoon toasted sesame oil
- 1 teaspoon minced garlic
- 4 large eggs, beaten
- Sea salt to taste
- Freshly ground black pepper to taste
- 2 scallions, trimmed and chopped
- 24 to 30 dumpling, gyoza, or potsticker wrappers

1. To a hot wok, add the vegetable oil and sesame oil. Add the garlic and cook for about 30 seconds.
2. Add the eggs to the wok, and season with the sea salt and pepper to taste. Scramble the eggs with a heat-proof spatula for about 30 seconds, or until done. Add the scallions and mix with the scrambled eggs. Transfer the eggs to a plate, and set aside to cool until they can be handled.
3. Spoon a heaping teaspoon of the egg and scallion filling into the center of a dumpling wrapper. Wet the edges of the wrapper with water, fold the wrapper to enclose the filling, and seal the dumpling by pinching the wrapper at its edges. Repeat with the remaining wrappers and filling. Make sure the uncooked dumplings don't touch each other. They will stick together until they're cooked.
4. Steam, pan-fry, boil, or deep-fry the dumplings, or use them in soup.

Spicy Shrimp with Ginger Dumplings

Prep time: 10 minutes | Cook time: 8 minutes | Serves 4

- ½ pound (227g) raw shrimp, peeled, deveined
- 1 teaspoon oyster sauce
- 1 tablespoon vegetable oil
- ¼ teaspoon white pepper
- 1 teaspoon sesame oil
- ¼ teaspoon salt
- 1 teaspoon sugar
- ½ teaspoon ginger, minced
- ¼ cup bamboo shoots, chopped
- 12 dumpling wrappers

1. Blend shrimp with all the filling ingredients (except bamboo shoots) in a blender. Add bamboo shoots to the blended filling and mix well. Cover and refrigerate this filling for 1 hour.
2. Meanwhile, spread the dumpling wrappers on the working surface. Divide the shrimp filling at the center of each dumpling wrapper. Wet the edges of the dumplings and bring all the edges of each dumpling together. Pinch and seal the edges of the dumplings to seal the filling inside.
3. Boil water in a suitable pot with a steamer basket placed inside.
4. Add the dumplings to the steamer, cover and steam for 6 minutes.
5. Meanwhile, heat about 2 tablespoons oil in a Mandarin wok.
6. Sear the dumpling for 2 minutes until golden.
7. Serve warm.

Scallion with Steamed Egg Custard

Prep time: 10 minutes | Cook time: 10 minutes | Serves 4

- 4 large eggs, at room temperature
- 1¾ cups low-sodium chicken broth or filtered water
- 2 teaspoons Shaoxing rice wine
- ½ teaspoon kosher salt
- 2 scallions, green part only, thinly sliced
- 4 teaspoons sesame oil

1. In a large bowl, whisk the eggs. Add the broth and rice wine and whisk to combine. Strain the egg mixture through a fine-mesh sieve set over a liquid measuring cup to remove air bubbles. Pour the egg mixture into 4 (6-ounce / 170-g) ramekins. With a paring knife, pop any bubbles on the surface of the egg mixture. Cover the ramekins with aluminum foil.
2. Rinse a bamboo steamer basket and its lid under cold water and place it in the wok. Pour in 2 inches of water, or until it comes above the bottom rim of the steamer by ¼ to ½ inch, but not so much that it touches the bottom of the basket. Place the ramekins in the steamer basket. Cover with the lid.
3. Bring the water to a boil, then reduce the heat to a low simmer. Steam over low heat for about 10 minutes or until the eggs are just set.
4. Carefully remove the ramekins from the steamer and garnish each custard with some scallions and a few drops of sesame oil. Serve immediately.

Spiced Turmeric Popcorn with Cinnamon

Prep time: 15 minutes | Cook time: 10 minutes | Serves 4

FOR THE SPICE BLEND:

- 1 whole star anise, seeds removed and husks discarded
- 6 green cardamom pods, seeds removed and husks discarded
- 4 whole cloves
- 4 black peppercorns
- 1 teaspoon coriander seeds
- 1 teaspoon fennel seeds
- 1 teaspoon ground cinnamon
- 1 teaspoon ground ginger
- ½ teaspoon ground turmeric
- ⅛ teaspoon ground cayenne pepper
- For the Popcorn:
- 2 tablespoons vegetable oil
- ½ cup popcorn kernels
- Kosher salt to taste

SPICE BLEND

1. In a small sauté pan or skillet, combine the star anise seeds, cardamom seeds, cloves, peppercorns, coriander seeds, and fennel seeds. Heat the skillet over medium heat and gently shake and swirl the spices around the pan. Toast the spices for 5 to 6 minutes, or until you can smell the spices and they start to pop.
2. Remove the pan from the heat and transfer the spices to a mortar and pestle or spice grinder. Cool the spices for 2 minutes before grinding. Grind the spices to a fine powder and transfer to a small bowl.
3. Add the ground cinnamon, ginger, turmeric, and cayenne pepper and stir to combine. Set aside.

POPCORN

4. Heat a wok over medium-high heat until it just begins to smoke. Pour in the vegetable oil and ghee and swirl to coat the wok. Add 2 popcorn kernels to the wok and cover. Once they pop, add the rest of the kernels and cover. Shake constantly until the popping stops and remove from the heat.
5. Transfer the popcorn to a large paper bag. Add 2 generous pinches of kosher salt and 1½ tablespoons of the spice blend. Fold the bag closed and shake! Pour into a large bowl and enjoy immediately.

Brothy Gravy with Egg Foo Young

Prep time: 10 minutes | Cook time: 10 minutes | Serves 4

FOR THE GRAVY:

- ¾ cup chicken broth
- 1½ tablespoons hoisin sauce
- 1 tablespoon cornstarch dissolved in 2 tablespoons cold water
- For the Egg Foo Young:
- 3 to 3½ tablespoons peanut or vegetable oil, divided
- 3 or 4 shiitake or cremini mushrooms, thinly sliced
- 4 scallions, thinly sliced
- 1½ cups fresh bean sprouts
- ¼ cup chopped ham or Canadian bacon
- 1½ teaspoons soy sauce
- 1 teaspoon sesame oil
- 6 large eggs

1. Heat a wok over medium-high heat until a drop of water sizzles on contact. Add 1 tablespoon of peanut oil, and swirl to coat the bottom of the wok.
2. Add the shiitake mushrooms, scallions, and bean sprouts to the wok, and Stir-frythem for about 3 minutes. Add the ham, soy sauce, and sesame oil to the wok, and Stir-frythem for another 1 to 2 minutes. Remove the filling mixture from the wok and set it aside.
3. In a medium bowl, beat the eggs. Add the filling mixture to the eggs and mix to combine.
4. Heat the wok to medium-high, and add 1 tablespoon of peanut oil. Pour in one quarter of the egg mixture to make an omelet. Cook the egg mixture until it is golden brown, 1 to 2 minutes per side. Transfer the omelet to a plate. Repeat this step with the rest of the egg mixture to make a total of 4 omelets. For each subsequent omelet, use only 1½ teaspoons or less of the remaining peanut oil.
5. To serve, pour some gravy over each omelet.

Eggy Almond Sponge Cake
Prep time: 10 minutes | Cook time: 20 minutes | Makes 8

- Nonstick cooking spray
- 1 cup cake flour, sifted
- 1 teaspoon baking powder
- ¼ teaspoon kosher salt
- 5 large eggs, separated
- ¾ cup sugar, divided
- 1 teaspoon almond extract
- ½ teaspoon cream of tartar

1. Line an 8-inch cake pan with parchment paper. Lightly spray the parchment with nonstick cooking spray and set aside.
2. Into a bowl, sift the cake flour, baking powder, and salt together.
3. In a stand mixer or hand mixer on medium, beat the egg yolks with ½ cup of sugar and the almond extract for about 3 minutes, until pale and thick. Add the flour mixture and mix until just combined. Set aside.
4. Clean the whisk and in another clean bowl, whip the egg whites with the cream of tartar until frothy. While the mixer is running, continue to whisk the whites while gradually adding the remaining ¼ cup of sugar. Beat for 4 to 5 minutes, until the whites turn shiny and develop stiff peaks.
5. Fold the egg whites into the cake batter and gently combine until the egg whites are incorporated. Transfer the batter to the prepared cake pan.
6. Rinse a bamboo steamer basket and its lid under cold water and place it in the wok. Pour in 2 inches of water, or until it comes above the bottom rim of the steamer by ¼ to ½ inch, but not so much that it touches the bottom of the basket. Set the center pan in the steamer basket.
7. Bring the water to a boil over high heat. Place the cover on the steamer basket and turn the heat down to medium. Steam the cake for 25 minutes, or until a toothpick inserted into the center comes out clean.
8. Transfer the cake to a wire cooling rack and cool for 10 minutes. Turn the cake out onto the rack and remove the parchment paper. Invert the cake back onto a serving plate so that it is right side up. Slice into 8 wedges and serve warm.

Buttered Egg Puffs
Prep time: 10 minutes | Cook time: 20 minutes | Makes 8

- ½ cup water
- 2 teaspoons unsalted butter
- ¼ cup sugar, divided
- Kosher salt to taste
- ½ cup all-purpose unbleached flour
- 3 cups vegetable oil
- 2 large eggs, beaten

1. In a small saucepan, heat the water, butter, 2 teaspoons of sugar, and a pinch of salt to taste over medium-high heat. Bring to a boil and stir in the flour. Continue stirring the flour with a wooden spoon until the mixture looks like mashed potatoes and a thin film of dough has developed on the bottom of the pan. Turn off the heat and transfer the dough to a large mixing bowl. Cool the dough for about 5 minutes, stirring occasionally.
2. While the dough cools, pour the oil into the wok; the oil should be about 1 to 1½ inches deep. Bring the oil to 375°F (190°C) over medium-high heat. You can tell the oil is ready when you dip the end of a wooden spoon in and the oil bubbles and sizzles around the spoon.
3. Pour the beaten eggs into the dough in two batches, vigorously stirring the eggs into the dough before adding the next batch. When all the eggs have been incorporated, the batter should look satiny and shiny.
4. Using 2 tablespoons, scoop the batter with one and use the other to gently nudge the batter off the spoon into the hot oil. Let the puffs fry for 8 to 10 minutes, flipping often, until the puffs swell to 3 times their original size and turn golden brown and crispy.
5. Using a wok skimmer, transfer the puffs to a paper towel–lined plate and cool for 2 to 3 minutes. Place the remaining sugar in a bowl and toss the puffs in it. Serve warm.

Sugar with Caramel Granola

Prep time: 10 minutes | Cook time: 5 minutes | Serves 8

- 2 cups of quick-boiling oats
- 1 cup of brown sugar
- 2 tablespoons of ground cinnamon
- ½ cup melted butter
- 5 tablespoons of caramel sauce
- 2 tablespoons of white sugar

1. Mix the oats, brown sugar and cinnamon in a wok or a large pan over high heat, cook for 5 to 10 minutes; remove from heat and add butter and caramel sauce; stir evenly.
2. Spread the mixture in a thin layer on a flat plate or baking sheet. Sprinkle the white sugar over the muesli. Let cool completely before serving.

Sugared Dessert Soup

Prep time: 10 minutes | Cook time: 10 minutes | Serves 4

- 3 cups water
- ¾ cup granulated sugar
- ¼ cup light brown sugar
- 2-inch fresh ginger piece, peeled and smashed
- 1 tablespoon dried chrysanthemum buds
- 2 large yellow peaches, peeled, pitted, and sliced into 8 wedges each

1. In a wok over high heat, bring the water to a boil, then lower the heat to medium-low and add the granulated sugar, brown sugar, ginger, and chrysanthemum buds. Stir gently to dissolve the sugars. Add the peaches.
2. Simmer gently for 10 to 15 minutes, or until the peaches are tender. They may impart a beautiful rosy color to the soup. Discard the ginger and divide the soup and peaches into bowls and serve.

Milky Mango Pudding

Prep time: 5 minutes | Cook time: 0 minutes | Serves 4

- ½ pound frozen mango chunks
- ¼ cup sugar
- ½ cup hot water
- 1 packet unflavored gelatin
- ½ cup evaporated milk
- Raspberries or kiwi slices, for garnish (optional)

1. In a blender, purée the mango and sugar until smooth.
2. In a large bowl, mix the hot water and gelatin. Let it stand for a few minutes.
3. Add the evaporated milk to the gelatin, and stir until they are combined. Add the mango purée and mix until well combined.
4. Pour the pudding into individual small cups or ramekins. Cover each one with plastic wrap, and chill in the refrigerator for at least 2 hours.
5. Before serving, garnish each pudding with the raspberries or kiwi (if using).

Sugar and Vinegar with Cucumber Salad

Prep time: 10 minutes | Cook time: 2 minutes | Serves 4

- 6 garlic cloves, minced
- 3 tablespoons oil
- 2 English cucumbers, sliced
- 1½ teaspoon salt
- 1 teaspoon sugar
- ⅛ teaspoon MSG
- ¼ teaspoon sesame oil
- 1 tablespoon rice vinegar

1. Sauté garlic with oil in a Cantonese wok for 30 seconds.
2. Stir in sugar, MSG, sesame oil, rice vinegar, and salt.
3. Cook for 1 minute, then toss in cucumber.
4. Mix well and serve.

Milky Coconut and Peanut Mochi

Prep time: 10 minutes | Cook time: 18 minutes | Serve 14

FOR THE DOUGH:

- 1½ cups sweet rice flour
- ¼ cup cornstarch
- ¼ cup caster sugar
- 1 ½ cups coconut milk
- 2 tablespoons coconut oil
- For the Filling:
- ½ cup peanuts
- ½ cup coconut flakes, chopped
- 3 tablespoons sugar
- 1 tablespoon melted coconut oil
- For the Coconut Peanut Mochi:
- A large piece of wax paper
- 1 cup coconut flakes, chopped
- 16 small paper cupcake cups

1. Add peanuts to a Mandarin wok and roast them for 3 to 5 minutes until golden-brown.
2. Allow the peanuts to cool, then chop them finely.
3. Layer a 11-inch by 11-inch cake pan with wax paper and brush with vegetable oil.
4. Whisk rice flour, sugar, cornstarch, coconut oil, and coconut milk in a bowl.
5. Boil water in a suitable cooking pot, place the steam rack inside and add the dough in the steamer.
6. Cover and cook for 15 minutes in the steamer then allow the dough to cool.
7. Meanwhile, mix peanuts with 1 tablespoon coconut oil, sugar, and coconut flakes in a bowl.
8. Spread the prepared dough in the prepared pan and cut it into 14 squares.
9. Add a tablespoon the filling at the center of each square.
10. Pinch the edges of each square and roll it into a ball.
11. Coat all the balls with coconut flakes and place them in the cupcake cup.
12. Leave them for 20 minutes.
13. Serve.

Cabbage with Spicy Potstickers

Prep time: 15 minutes | Cook time: 3 minutes | Serves 6

- ½ pound (227g) ground pork
- 1 cup finely shredded cabbage
- 2 scallions, sliced
- 2 teaspoons minced ginger
- 2 tablespoons soy sauce
- 1 teaspoon sesame oil
- ½ teaspoon pepper
- 24 dumpling skins
- 2 tablespoons vegetable oil
- ¼ cup water
- ¼ cup chopped scallions

1. In a large bowl, combine the pork, cabbage, scallions, ginger, soy sauce, sesame oil, and pepper. Refrigerate for 30 minutes.
2. Take 1 dumpling skin and use your finger to brush water along the edge of the circle. Place about 1 tablespoon of the mixture in the center of the skin. Fold the dumpling skin over and firmly press the sides to seal completely. While you are forming the potstickers, create a flattened bottom. You can also pleat the edges if you like.
3. Heat the oil in a wok over medium heat. Place the potstickers, flattened side down, in one layer and fry for 1 to 2 minutes.
4. Carefully pour the water into the wok and cover. Allow the pot stickers to steam for an additional 2 to 3 minutes. Remove the lid and continue cooking until the water has evaporated.
5. Place the potstickers on a plate and sprinkle the tops with scallions. Serve hot.

Limey Parsley Calamari

Prep time: 10 minutes | Cook time: 2 minutes | Serves 4

- ½ cup Tequila Lime Marinade
- 1 pound (454 g) calamari tubes, cut into 1 pieces
- 2 tablespoons vegetable oil
- 1 tablespoon lime juice
- 2 tablespoons extra-virgin olive oil
- 2 tablespoons chopped Italian parsley
- ½ teaspoon kosher salt

1. Combine the marinade with the calamari in a large bowl. Refrigerate for 5 minutes.
2. Heat a wok to medium-high heat and add the vegetable oil. Swirl the oil around the wok and add the calamari. Toss and Stir-frythe calamari for 2 to 3 minutes.
3. Remove the calamari to a plate and drizzle with lime juice, olive oil, and parsley. Season with salt to taste and serve immediately.

Carrots and Scallion Egg Rolls

Prep time: 15 minutes | Cook time: 5 minutes | Makes 12

- 1 pound (454 g) lean ground pork
- 1 tablespoon dark soy sauce
- 2 tablespoons oyster sauce
- 1 teaspoon minced garlic, divided
- 1 teaspoon minced ginger, divided
- 1 cup shredded carrots
- 2 scallions, finely chopped
- 1 teaspoon sesame oil
- 1 teaspoon black pepper
- 25 (6 × 6) egg roll wrappers
- 2 eggs, beaten
- 2 cups peanut or vegetable oil

1. In a large bowl, mix together the ground pork, soy sauce, oyster sauce, garlic, ginger, carrots, scallions, and sesame oil. Add the black pepper.
2. One at a time, place an eggroll wrapper on a flat surface with one of the points facing toward you. Spoon about 2 tablespoons of the filling in a line toward the bottom half of the wrapper. Brush the top corner and sides with the beaten egg. Fold in the sides of the wrapper and tightly roll the egg roll up until it is closed. Press to seal, set aside, and continue with the remaining ingredients.
3. Heat the oil in a wok over high heat to 375°F (190°C). In batches, fry the egg rolls until golden brown, about 5 to 6 minutes. Remove the fried egg rolls to plates lined with paper towels to drain. Serve hot.

Kirana's Okra Stir-fry
Prep time: 15 minutes | Cook time: 15 minutes | Serves 4

- 2 tablespoons of vegetable oil
- 450 g small okra
- 1/2 teaspoon of ground turmeric
- 1 clove of chopped garlic
- 1/2 teaspoon of chopped fresh ginger
- 2 quartered onions
- 2 quartered romaine tomatoes
- 1 tablespoon of chopped fresh coriander

1. Heat a large pan or wok with vegetable oil on medium to high heat, add the okra, and Stir-fryfor 3 minutes until soft and golden brown.
2. Place the stir-fried okra on a plate.
3. Add turmeric to the hot oil and heat it for 1-2 minutes or until it smells fragrant.
4. Mix in the ginger, tomatoes, onions and garlic and Stir-fryfor about 10 minutes until the onions are soft.
5. Add the stir-fried okra to the onion mixture.
6. Garnish with coriander.

Chicken and Snow Peas Stir-fry
Prep time: 15 minutes | Cook time: 15 minutes | Serves 6

- 1 cup of chicken broth
- 3 tablespoons of soy sauce
- 1 tablespoon of cornstarch
- 1 tablespoon of ground ginger
- 2 tablespoons of vegetable oil
- 4 large skin and bone halves of chicken breast, cut into cubes
- 2 cloves of garlic, chopped
- 1 1/2 cups sliced fresh mushrooms
- 2 (225 g cans of sliced and drained water chestnuts
- 3 cups of sugar peas
- 1 tablespoon of sesame seeds

1. Whisk the chicken stock, cornstarch, soy sauce and ginger in a small bowl and set aside. In a large pan or wok, heat the oil and fry the chicken and garlic for 8-10 minutes until the chicken is cooked through.
2. Add the water chestnuts, mushrooms and the reserved chicken broth mixture while stirring. Cook for 3-5 minutes until the sauce starts to thicken.
3. Add the sugar snap peas to the pan while stirring and cook for 3-5 minutes until tender.
4. 4. Place on a plate or platter, sprinkle with sesame seeds and serve.

Honey Beef Stir-fry
Prep time: 20 minutes | Cook time: 25 minutes | Serves 4

- 1/3 cup soy sauce
- 1/2 teaspoon sesame oil
- 1 tablespoon of honey
- 1 clove of garlic (finely chopped or grated)
- 1 teaspoon fresh ginger (finely chopped or grated
- 1 teaspoon cornstarch
- 1 teaspoon of water
- 450 g boneless sirloin, flank or rock steak cut into strips
- 1 package (400 g frozen or fresh broccoli florets
- 3 teaspoons of vegetable oil

1. Mix honey, soy sauce, sesame oil, ginger and garlic together. In a Ziploc plastic bag (or glass bowl, mix the beef and half of the sauce mixture together until the beef is coated.
2. Set the marinade aside for 20 minutes or keep covered in the refrigerator overnight. Mix the water and cornstarch and add to the remaining sauce mixture.
3. Heat a large pan or wok with 2 teaspoons of oil over high heat and add the marinated beef. Cook for 4 minutes and then transfer the cooked beef to a clean bowl.
4. Put the remaining 1 teaspoon of oil in the wok, then add the broccoli and cook for 2 minutes. Return the cooked beef to the wok. Return the cooked beef to the wok.
5. Make a well in the middle and add the sauce. Cook the sauce for about 2 minutes or until the whole mixture is heated through and the sauce has thickened.
6. Serve with brown rice.

Chicken in Garlic and Black Bean Sauce
Prep time: 15 minutes | Cook time: 35 minutes | Serves 6

MARINADE:
- 1 tbsp cornstarch, 1 tbsp water and 1 tbsp soy sauce
- 1 1/2 teaspoons white sugar and 1 teaspoon salt
- 6 skinless and boned chicken halves (sliced)
- 1 cup of bean sprouts
- 1/4 cup of water

SAUCE:
- 2 teaspoons of oyster sauce and 1 tablespoon of white sugar
- 3 tbsp black bean sauce with garlic oyster sauce
- 1 teaspoon of white sugar
- 1 tablespoon of vegetable oil
- 3 tablespoons of black bean sauce with garlic
- 1 tablespoon of chopped garlic and 1 finely chopped onion
- 1/2 teaspoon salt and 1/2 chopped paprika
- 2 tablespoons of cornstarch and 1 tablespoon of water.

1. Mix one tablespoon each of water and cornstarch in a bowl. Stir in a teaspoon of salt, sugar and soy sauce;.Add the chicken. Mix well so that it combines. Set aside for marinating for 20 minutes.
2. Boil water in a saucepan. Add bean sprouts. Cook for half a minute until just blanched; Drain. In a small bowl, stir together the sugar, oyster sauce and a quarter cup of water.
3. Heat vegetable oil in a pan over high heat. Add the garlic and black bean sauce. Fry for 2-3 minutes, stirring, until flavorful. Add half a teaspoon of salt and the onion. Cook, stirring, for 3-4 minutes until tender; add the marinated chicken. Fry and stir for 3-4 minutes, until the chicken is cooked through and opaque.
4. Stir in the oyster sauce and cook for 1-2 minutes until it is cooked through; cover. Simmer for 3 minutes until the flavors have mixed. Cook peppers for 1-2 minutes, stirring until soft. Melt 2 teaspoons of cornstarch in a tablespoon of water. Fold in the bean sprouts and cornstarch mixture. Cook for another 2-3 minutes until the sauce is thick.

Cashew Chicken Stir-fry
Prep time: 25 minutes | Cook time: 15 minutes | Serves 4

- 4 skinless and boned chicken breast halves, cut into bite-sized pieces
- 1 tablespoon of Cajun spice mix or to taste
- 1 1/4 cups of chicken broth
- 1 tablespoon of cornstarch
- 4 teaspoons of soy sauce
- 2 tablespoons of olive oil, divided
- 2 cups of shredded cabbage
- 25 chopped snow peas
- 10 small sticks of fresh asparagus, cut into bite-sized pieces
- 3 stalks of chopped celery
- 1/2 red bell pepper, cut into thin strips
- 2 green onions, chopped
- 1 can of cut and drained bamboo shoots
- 1/2 cup cashew nuts
- 1 pinch of paprika, or to taste (optional

1. Sprinkle Cajun seasoning over the chicken pieces. In a bowl, stir together 3 tablespoons of soy sauce, cornstarch and chicken stock until everything is well mixed.
2. Heat a tablespoon of olive oil in a wok or deep pan over high heat. Fry the chicken in the hot oil for 6-10 minutes, until completely cooked. Take the chicken out of the pan and pour off the accumulated liquid.
3. Heat the remaining 1 tablespoon of olive oil in a wok or pan over high heat. Fry and stir together bamboo shoots, cabbage, green onions, snow peas, red peppers, asparagus and celery for a minute; add a teaspoon of soy sauce.
4. Cook for 3 minutes until the vegetables are crispy and tender. Mix the chicken into the cabbage mixture then add the chicken broth to the chicken mixture.
5. Switch to medium heat and let it simmer for a minute until the sauce is thick. Turn on low heat then add the cashews; cook another minute until completely heated. Top with paprika.

Beef and Napa Cabbage Stir-fry

Prep time: 15 minutes | Cook time: 10 minutes | Serves 2

- 1 tablespoon of soy sauce
- 1 tablespoon rice vinegar (not seasoned)
- 2 tablespoons of oyster sauce
- 1 tablespoon of cornstarch
- 450 g flank steak
- 3 tablespoons of vegetable oil, divided
- 3 cloves of crushed garlic
- 1 piece of peeled and sliced ginger
- 450 g Napa cabbage, leaves and stems separated as desired, then cut into pieces
- Garnish: chopped shallot

1. Combine oyster sauce, soy sauce, corn starch and vinegar. Pat the steak dry and cut it in half lengthways, then cut it across into slices. Season with 1 teaspoon of pepper and 1/2 teaspoon of salt.
2. Heat a wok over high heat until a drop of water drips onto the cooking surface of the wok and the water evaporates immediately. Pour in 2 tablespoons of vegetable oil and swirl over the wok.
3. Fry the ginger and garlic for about 30 seconds until they are golden brown and fragrant. Add the beef and quickly place the beef slices in 1 layer around the wok. Cook for 2 minutes without stirring and then fry for about 1 minute, stirring, until the meat is brown on the outside but pink on the inside.
4. Put in a bowl. Wipe the wok clean and toss the remaining tablespoons of oil into the wok over high heat. Fry the cabbage stalks for about 2 minutes while stirring until they are tenderly crispy.
5. Add the cooked beef with the juice and cabbage leaves to the soy mixture and mix well. Fry the mixture for 1-2 minutes, stirring, until the sauce simmer and is slightly thick.
6. Throw away the ginger if you want. Season to taste with salt.

Summer Vegetable Stir-fry with Couscous

Prep time: 10 minutes | Cook time: 15 minutes | Serves 4

- 2 cups of diced peeled eggplant
- 1 1/2 teaspoons of salt
- 1 1/2 cups of water
- 1 cup of couscous
- 2 1/2 tablespoons of rapeseed oil
- 2 1/2 tablespoons of red wine vinegar
- 1 cup of diced peeled carrots
- 1 cup of diced zucchini
- 1 cup of diced yellow tortoiseshell squash
- 1 cup small broccoli florets
- 1 cup of diced red pepper
- 1/2 cup of diced red onion
- 2 cloves of chopped garlic
- 4 tablespoons of chopped fresh basil
- 2 tablespoons of chopped fresh mint
- 2 tablespoons of toasted pine nuts

1. Put eggplant and 1 teaspoon salt in a medium bowl; Let stand for 30 minutes. Rinse and drain eggplant. Pat dry. Bring 1 1/2 cups of water and 1/2 teaspoon of salt to a boil in a large saucepan; Stir in the couscous.
2. Take off the stove. Cover and let stand for 10 minutes. Discover; Shake up with a fork. Whisk 1 1/2 tablespoons of oil and vinegar in a small bowl.
3. Heat 1 tablespoon of oil in a wok or in a large nonstick pan over medium to high heat. Add eggplants and carrots; Fry for 3 minutes while stirring.
4. Add zucchini and the next 5 ingredients; Fry while stirring until the vegetables are crispy and tender, about 2 minutes. Add the couscous and vinegar mixture; Fry for 1 minute while stirring.
5. Stir in basil and mint.
6. Season with salt and pepper.

Vegetarian Thai Fried Rice Khao Pad Je
Prep time: 15 minutes | Cook time: 10 minutes | Serves 4

- 2 tablespoons of vegetable oil, or more as needed
- 1/2 onion, chopped 9 ounces firm tofu, crumbled
- 1 cup of peas
- 1 cup of chopped tomatoes
- 4 cups of cooked jasmine rice
- 2 tablespoons of light soy sauce
- 2 teaspoons of dark sweet soy sauce
- 3 eggs
- 1 teaspoon of liquid soy-based spice
- 1 cup drained pineapple pieces
- 1/4 teaspoon of ground white pepper

1. Heat 1 tablespoon of vegetable oil in a wok or large pan over high heat. Cook the onion and tofu for 3 to 5 minutes, until lightly browned. Add peas and tomatoes and cook for 1 minute.
2. Stir in rice and possibly a little more oil so that the rice doesn't burn. Fry for 1 minute while stirring. Season with light soy sauce and sweet soy sauce; mix well.
3. Place rice on one side of the wok or pan and put 1 tablespoon of vegetable oil on the empty side.
4. Beat eggs in the pan and season with soy seasoning. Let the eggs boil for about 3 minutes; turn over and stir. Stir into the rice mixture; Stir in pineapple until warmed through.
5. Season with white pepper. Season to taste and adjust the seasoning if necessary.

Vegetarian Congee Xifan
Prep time: 15 minutes | Cook time: 10 minutes | Serves 4

- 2 tablespoons of vegetable oil
- 2 cloves of crushed and finely chopped garlic
- 1 tablespoon of freshly grated ginger
- 6 dried Chinese mushrooms, soaked in hot water for 20 minutes, stems discarded, finely chopped
- 1 small carrot, diced
- 1 cup of brown basmati rice
- 1 cup of equal parts green split peas, whole green lentils, whole grains, barley flakes and pearl barley
- 12 cups of boiling water
- 1 red pepper, finely diced
- 4 cups of vegetable broth
- Handful of canned and chopped bamboo shoots
- 2 tablespoons of light soy sauce
- 1 tablespoon of toasted sesame oil
- Freshly ground black pepper
- Small handfuls of chopped coriander leaves and stalks

1. Fry the garlic and ginger and the Chinese mushrooms for less than 1 minute while stirring. Add the carrot, brown rice, and whole grain mixture.
2. Fry for less than 1 minute while stirring and add 4 cups of boiling water. Cook for 25-30 minutes, stirring, and adding another 8 cups of water to make sure the rice and grains are well cooked.

3. Add the red pepper, stir well then pour in the vegetable stock. Finally, add the bamboo shoots and season with the light soy sauce, sesame oil and ground black pepper.
4. Sprinkle with the chopped coriander and serve immediately.

Stir-fry Cabbage
Prep time: 10 minutes | Cook time: 5 minutes | Serves 4

- 1 tablespoon of vegetable oil
- 2 cloves of garlic, chopped
- 450 g of chopped cabbage
- 1 tablespoon of soy sauce
- 1 tablespoon of Chinese cooking wine (Shaoxing wine)

1. Heat the vegetable oil in a wok or large pan over medium heat. Stir in the garlic and cook for a few seconds until it begins to brown.
2. Stir in the cabbage until it is covered in oil; cover the wok and cook for 1 minute.
3. Add the soy sauce and cook for another minute and stir. Turn the heat on high and stir in the Chinese cooking wine.
4. Cook and stir until the cabbage is tender, about 2 more minutes.

Spicy Pork and Cashew Stir-fry with Snow Peas

Prep time: 45 minutes | Cook time: 45 minutes | Serves 4

- 1 tablespoon of semi-dry sherry
- 2 teaspoons of cornstarch
- 3 tablespoons of soy sauce
- 2 teaspoons of Asian sesame oil
- 350 g boneless pork loin (thinly sliced then cut into strips
- 1 teaspoon of sugar
- 3 tablespoons of peanut oil
- 2 teaspoons of chopped peeled fresh ginger
- 2 teaspoons of minced garlic
- 1/2 teaspoon dried hot red pepper flakes
- 1 large red pepper, cut into strips
- 225 g snow peas (trimmed
- 1 cup of salted roasted cashew nuts

1. Mix sherry, cornstarch and 1 tablespoon soy sauce, then stir in sesame oil. Add the pork while stirring, stir well and let stand for 10 minutes. Mix the sugar and the remaining 2 tablespoons of soy sauce.
2. Heat a wok or a large non-stick pan over high heat. Add 1 1/2 tablespoons of peanut oil, toss the wok until it is evenly covered, then fry 1 teaspoon of ginger, 1 teaspoon of garlic, and 1/4 teaspoon of pepper flakes, stirring until fragrant, about 5 seconds.
3. Add paprika and Stir-fry for 2 minutes. Add snow peas and cashew nuts and Stir-fry until the peas are crispy and tender (1 to 2 minutes. Transfer the vegetables to a bowl. Heat 1 1/2 tablespoons of peanut oil in a wok until it is just smoked, then fry the remaining ginger, garlic and pepper flakes while stirring until they are fragrant, about 5 seconds.
4. Add the pork and Stir Fry, separating the strips until they are browned and barely cooked through, 2 to 3 minutes. Add the vegetables and sweetened soy sauce, then Stir-fry until the vegetables are just cooked through, about 1 minute longer.

Baby Bok Choy Stir-fry

Prep time: 15 minutes | Cook time: 15 minutes | Serves 4

- 600 g baby bok choy
- 2 tablespoons of peanut oil
- 1 piece of fresh ginger, chopped (about 1 teaspoon
- 2 spring onions (white and green parts, thinly sliced
- 4 cloves of garlic, thinly sliced
- 1 teaspoon of coarse sea or kosher salt
- 1 teaspoon of sugar
- 1/8 teaspoon of ground white pepper

1. Cut a piece off the end of each bok choy head. Cut the bok choy crosswise into slices. Wash the bok choy with cold water in several passes and dry in a colander or salad spinner until dry to the touch.
2. Heat the oil in a wok or in a large pan over moderate heat until it is hot, but not smoking. Add ginger, spring onions and garlic and Stir-fry until flavored, about 15 seconds.
3. Add bok choy, salt, sugar and pepper and Stir-fry for 1 minute. Add 1 tablespoon of water, cover and cook, covered, for about 30 seconds until they are wilted.
4. Uncover, Stir-fry for 5 seconds, then cover again, turn off the flame and let it simmer in the residual heat until just soft, about 30 seconds longer.

Spicy Fried Brown Rice with Broccolini and Scallops

Prep time: 10 minutes | Cook time: 15 minutes | Serves 4

- 1/2 cup of water
- 225 g broccolini, cut into pieces (about 3 cups
- 1 tablespoon of vegetable oil
- 1 cup of diced red pepper
- 1 cup chopped green onions
- 1 tablespoon of chopped fresh peeled ginger
- 2 cloves of chopped garlic
- 1/4 teaspoon dried crushed red pepper
- 340 g of bay leaves
- 1 1/2 cup of brown basmati rice or other brown rice (cooked, drained, chilled
- 2 tablespoons of soy sauce
- 2 teaspoons of oriental sesame oil

1. Bring 1/2 cup of water to a boil in a large pan over medium-high heat. Add broccolini; Cover and cook for approx. 3 minutes until crispy and tender.
2. Let it drain. Heat the oil in the same pan over high heat. Add the next 5 ingredients; Stir for 30 seconds. Move vegetables to the side of the pan; Place the scallops on the other side.
3. Sprinkle with salt and pepper; Fry for 1 minute while stirring. Stir the vegetables into the scallops. Add rice, broccolini, soy sauce and sesame oil and Stir-fry for about 2 minutes until everything is heated.
4. Season with salt and pepper.

Delicious Stir-fry Rice

Prep time: 10 minutes | Cook time: 25 minutes | Serves 4

- 2 1/4 cups of water
- 1 1/2 cup long grain white rice
- 2 1/2 tablespoons of vegetable oil
- 4 eggs, beaten into a mixture
- 2 carrots, peeled, thinly sliced diagonally, then sliced
- 3 cups thinly sliced bok choy stems and leaves
- 100 g fresh shiitake mushrooms (stems removed and hats sliced
- 110 peas, (cut, sliced)
- 1 1/2 tablespoons of oriental sesame oil
- 3 green onions (sliced
- Szechuan salt and pepper

FOR RICE:

1. Bring 2 1/4 cups of water to a boil in a medium saucepan, add rice and bring to a boil. Reduce heat to low, cover and cook until water is absorbed, about 20 minutes. Shake with a fork. Transfer to a bowl and let cool completely. It can be made 1 day in advance. Heat 1 1/2 tablespoons of vegetable oil in a wok or in a heavy large pan over high heat until it is hot but not smoking. Add eggs and cook until puffed on the edge.
2. Use a spatula to push the boiled egg towards the back of the pan while tilting the pan forward so that the uncooked egg can flow forward. Continue cooking until the eggs are no longer runny, but rather soft and fluffy. Cut the eggs into pieces with the edge of the spatula and place on the plate. Heat 1 tablespoon of vegetable oil in a wok over high heat. Cut the carrots into slices and Stir-fry for 1 minute.
3. Add sliced bok choy, sliced shiitake mushroom caps and sliced snow peas. Sprinkle with salt and pepper and Stir-fry until the vegetables just soften, about 4 minutes. Add oriental sesame oil and heat the mixture, then add the cooked rice and Stir-fry until it is completely heated. Stir in eggs and sliced green onions. Season the rice with Szechuan salt and pepper and serve immediately.

Pork Stir-fry

Prep time: 30 minutes | Cook time: 10 minutes | Serves 2

- 6 leaves of lettuce (stem lettuce, cut into pieces
- 1 pinch of salt
- 2 teaspoons of water
- 1 teaspoon cornstarch
- 225 grams of lean pork, cut into cubes
- 1 teaspoon rice wine
- 1/4 teaspoon salt
- 2 tablespoons of chicken broth
- 2 teaspoons of soy sauce
- 1/2 teaspoon Chinese black vinegar
- 1/2 teaspoon white sugar
- 3 1/2 tablespoons of vegetable oil
- 1 tablespoon of finely chopped pickled red chilies
- 2 teaspoons of chili bean sauce
- 3 diced spring onions
- 2 cloves of sliced garlic
- 1 piece of sliced fresh ginger

1. Mix the lettuce and a pinch of salt in another bowl; mix the water and cornstarch in a small bowl; stir into a smooth paste; transfer half of the cornstarch paste to a larger bowl.
2. Add pork, rice wine and 1/4 teaspoon salt. In another bowl, whisk the remaining cornstarch paste, chicken broth, soy sauce, black vinegar, and sugar into a sauce and heat the oil in a wok or large pan over high heat.
3. Add pork with marinade; cook and stir for 3 to 4 minutes until browned. Stir in the pickled chili peppers and chili bean sauce; cook until the oil turns red, about 1 minute. Add green onions, garlic, and ginger; cook and stir until fragrant, about 1 minute.
4. Stir in the salad; Steam for 2 to 3 minutes until soft. Add the sauce and let it thicken while swirling continuously, about 3 minutes.

Sesame Pepper Stir-fry

Prep time: 20 minutes | Cook time: 15 minutes | Serves 4

- 1 small head of cabbage (thinly sliced)
- 2 red peppers (thinly sliced)
- 1 onion, sliced (optional)
- 8 cloves of garlic (finely diced)
- 4 teaspoons of grated fresh ginger
- 1/2 cup sesame oil, divided
- 450 gr. beef fillet (thinly sliced)
- 1/4 cup soy sauce
- 2 teaspoons of white sugar
- 1 teaspoon of ground black pepper
- 1 cup of water
- 4 teaspoons of cornstarch

1. Mix the cabbage and red bell pepper in a bowl. Mix the onion, garlic and ginger in a separate bowl. Heat a wok or large pan over medium-high heat. Add 1/4 cup of sesame oil.
2. Cook the beef and onion mixture in the hot oil and stir until the beef is browned on both sides for 3 to 4 minutes. Add the herb mixture to the beef mixture; Cook, stirring quickly, until the cabbage wilts, the onion begins to brown and the beef is completely cooked, about 5 minutes.
3. Stir 1/4 cup of sesame oil, soy sauce, sugar and black pepper into the beef and herb mixture; swivel to pull over. Mix the water and cornstarch in a bowl until the cornstarch is dissolved; add to the beef and cabbage mixture.
4. Cook and stir until the sauce reduces and thickens, about 5 minutes.

Bok Choy Stir-fry with Garlic

Prep time: 35 minutes | Cook time: 35 minutes | Serves 8

- 1/3 cup reduced sodium chicken broth
- 1 tablespoon of soy sauce
- 1 1/2 teaspoons of cornstarch
- 3 tablespoons of peanut or vegetable oil
- 1/4 cup thinly sliced garlic (about 8 cloves)
- 900 g Baby or Shanghai Bok Choy, halved lengthways
- 2 teaspoons of Asian sesame oil

1. Mix the stock, soy sauce, cornstarch and 1/2 teaspoon of salt together until the corn starch has dissolved. Stir over high heat until a drop of water evaporates immediately.
2. Pour peanut oil on the wok side, then swirl the oil and tilt the wok to coat the side. Add the garlic and Stir-fry for 5 to 10 seconds until the oil is pale golden.
3. Add half of the bok choy and Stir-fry until the leaves wilt, about 2 minutes then add the remaining bok choy and Stir-fry until all leaves are light green and limp, a total of 2 to 3 minutes.
4. Stir the stock mixture, then add to the wok and Stir-fry for 15 seconds. Cover with the lid and cook, stirring occasionally, until the vegetables are crispy and tender (2 to 4 minutes.

5. Stir in sesame oil then place on a serving plate. Cooks note: Baby Bok Choy can be washed, dried and cut in half 1 day in advance.
6. Wrapped in paper towels and refrigerated in a sealed bag

Brussels Sprouts with Garlic Stir-fry

Prep time: 10 minutes | Cook time: 15 minutes | Serves 4 - 6

- 4 cups halved Brussels sprouts kosher salt
- 1/4 cup vegetable oil
- 2 tablespoons of thinly sliced garlic
- 1/4 cup oyster sauce
- 4 teaspoons of Thai fish sauce (nam pla
- 2 teaspoons of soy sauce, preferably thin Thai soy sauce
- 2 teaspoons of sugar
- 1/2 teaspoon (or more sliced red Thai chili pods)
- Pinch of ground white pepper
- 1/2 cup low-salt chicken stock

1. Blanch the Brussels sprouts in a large saucepan with salted boiling water until they turn light green, about 15 seconds. Heat the oil in a wok or large pan over medium heat.
2. Add garlic and stir until light golden brown, about 30 seconds. Transfer to a small bowl with a slotted spoon. Increase heat to high level. Add Brussels sprouts.
3. Fry, stirring until they start to soften, 2-3 minutes. Add the oyster sauce and the next 5 ingredients. Fry for 30 seconds while stirring; Add chicken broth.
4. Bring to a boil; cook until the liquid is slightly reduced, about 2 minutes and add more chilies if desired. Stir in garlic.

Garlic Chives Stir-fry

Prep time: 10 minutes | Cook time: 10 minutes | Serves 4

- 1 tablespoon of peanut oil
- 300 g green garlic chives (also called Chinese chives; flat parts only, cut into pieces (4 cups)
- 1 teaspoon dried hot red pepper flakes
- 1/4 teaspoon salt, or to taste
- To serve: steamed white rice

1. Heat wok over high heat until a drop of water evaporates immediately on contact. Add oil to coat the wok evenly and heat until hot and only smoking.
2. Add chives and red pepper flakes and sauté while stirring, allowing the chives to rest on the bottom and sides of the wok for a few seconds between stirring operations, until soft and lightly browned, 2 to 4 minutes.
3. Stir in salt. Serve over rice.

Garlic Salad Stir-fry

Prep time: 10 minutes | Cook time: 10 minutes | Serves 4

- 1 tablespoon of Shaoxing rice wine or dry sherry
- 1 tablespoon of soy sauce
- 3/4 teaspoon sugar
- 1/2 teaspoon of salt
- 2 tablespoons of vegetable oil
- 5 medium-sized garlic cloves (crushed and peeled
- 450 g hearts of romaine lettuce (cut crosswise into pieces)
- 1 teaspoon sesame oil

1. Combine rice wine or sherry, soy sauce, sugar and salt in a small bowl and heat a flat-bottomed wok over high heat until a bead of water evaporates within 1 to 2 seconds of contact.
2. Stir in the vegetable oil, add the garlic and Stir-fry-for 5 seconds. Add the lettuce and Stir-fryfor 1 to 2 minutes or until just limp.
3. Stir the sauce, swirl it in the wok and fry for 30 seconds to 1 minute or until the salad is just soft and still light green.

Chinese Broccoli Stir-fry

Prep time: 10 minutes | Cook time: 15 minutes | Serves 4 - 6

- 3 tablespoons of vegetable oil
- 4 cloves of crushed garlic
- 900 g Chinese broccoli (sometimes known as Chinese cabbage, stem ends trimmed and broccoli cut into pieces)
- 1/2 cup of Thai chicken broth or canned chicken broth
- 2 tablespoons of Thai yellow bean sauce
- 2 tablespoons of oyster sauce
- 2 teaspoons of sugar

1. Heat the oil in the wok over high heat until it is hot but not smoked then fry the garlic, stirring, for 10 to 15 seconds until it is pale golden.
2. Add broccoli and broth and Stir-fryfor 2 minutes. Add the bean sauce, oyster sauce and sugar and Stir-fryfor 4 to 5 minutes until the broccoli is crispy and tender.

Pork Apple Stir-frywith Hoisin Sauce

Prep time: 20 minutes | Cook time: 20 minutes | Serves 3

- 2 tablespoons of hoisin sauce
- 2 tablespoons of brown sugar
- 6 tablespoons of soy sauce
- 1/2 cup apple sauce
- 450gr. pork loin, sliced and cut into thin strips
- 1 1/2 tablespoons of cornstarch
- 1/2 teaspoon sesame oil
- 1 tablespoon of chopped fresh ginger root
- 3 cups of broccoli florets

1. Whisk the hoisin sauce, brown sugar, soy sauce and apple sauce in a small bowl; Set aside and combine the pork and cornstarch in a bowl.
2. Heat the peanut oil and sesame oil in a large pan or heat in a wok over medium heat. Cook the pork in the hot oil in three separate batches until it is no longer pink in the middle, 2 to 3 minutes per batch.
3. Place the pork on a plate lined with paper towels to drain and save the oil. Add ginger to the pan, cook and stir for 30 seconds.
4. Stir in the broccoli and cook until tender. Return the pork to the pan and pour in the sauce; swivel to pull over. Cook until all ingredients are hot.

Coconut Curry Stir-fry

Prep time: 15 minutes | Cook time: 20 minutes | Serves 4

- 1 1/2 cups coconut milk
- 1 tablespoon of chopped ginger
- 1 tablespoon of lime juice
- 1 tablespoon of fish sauce
- 1 teaspoon of oyster sauce
- 2 teaspoons of minced garlic
- 1/2 teaspoon of chili garlic sauce
- 2 tablespoons of white sugar or sugar substitute
- 1 tablespoon of avocado oil
- 450 g chicken breast, cut into bite-sized pieces
- 1/2 onion, sliced
- 1 1/2 teaspoons of curry powder
- 2 cups of broccoli florets

1. Mix coconut milk, ginger, lime juice, fish sauce, oyster sauce, garlic, chili garlic sauce and sugar in a small bowl and heat the avocado oil in a large pan or in a wok over medium heat.
2. Fry the chicken in the hot oil while stirring until it is no longer pink (8 to 10 minutes. Take out of the wok and keep warm. Leave the remaining avocado oil in the pan.
3. Fry the onion and curry powder in hot oil in the pan for 2 minutes. Stir in broccoli; Fry for 3 minutes while stirring. Add coconut milk mixture and bring to a boil.
4. Reduce the heat to medium level and simmer the sauce and vegetables for 3 minutes. Return the chicken to the pan; Cook covered until the chicken is heated through and the vegetables are tender, about 3 minutes.

Essanaye's Sesame Beef Stir-fry

Prep time: 25 minutes | Cook time: approx. 8 hours | Serves 6

- 1/2 cup soy sauce
- 1/2 cup white sugar
- 1/3 cup rice wine vinegar
- 1/3 cup chopped garlic
- 1 tablespoon of sesame seeds
- 450 g thinly sliced steak
- 1/4 cup peanut oil
- 2 cups of sliced asparagus
- 1 cup of sliced fresh mushrooms or more to taste
- 1 chopped sweet onion
- 1 sliced red pepper
- 1 bunch of green onions (chopped into pieces
- 1 cup of whole cashews
- 1 tbsp sesame seeds
- 1 tbsp cornstarch (optional)
- 1 tbsp water (optional)
- 1 tbsp sesame seeds

1. Mix rice wine vinegar, soy sauce, 1 tablespoon of sesame seeds, garlic and sugar in a bowl and place the mixture in a zippered plastic bag. Pour the beef in, seal the bag and squeeze out as much air as you can, then gently massage the beef to evenly cover it with the marinade.
2. Heat a large pan or wok with peanut oil on medium to high heat and fry the marinated beef with the marinade for 5 minutes or until the beef is well browned.
3. Add the mushrooms, peppers, asparagus, spring onions and onions and cook for 3-4 minutes, stirring until the vegetables start to soften. Add 1 tablespoon of sesame seeds and cashew nuts and cook the mixture for another 2-3 minutes until the vegetables are soft.
4. Mix the water and cornstarch in a small bowl until the cornstarch is completely dissolved, then add it to the beef roast and cook the sauce for 3 minutes or until it is thick. Top with the remaining 1 tablespoon of sesame seeds.

Orange Ginger Shrimp Stir-fry

Prep time: 20 minutes | Cook time: 10 minutes | Serves 4

- 450 gr. Peeled and boned prawns
- 2 tablespoons of freshly squeezed orange juice
- 1 teaspoon of minced garlic
- 1 teaspoon of chopped fresh ginger root
- Salt and ground black pepper, to taste
- 1 tablespoon of vegetable oil
- 1 tablespoon of sesame oil
- 1 tablespoon of vegetable oil
- 1 diced green pepper
- 1 sliced yellow summer squash
- 1 cup of chopped broccoli
- 1/2 cup diced onion
- 1/2 cup chopped orange carrot, with peel
- 1/4 teaspoon cayenne pepper
- 1 1/2 cup cooked rice

1. Mix the shrimp, orange juice, garlic and ginger in a bowl; Season with salt and pepper. Put in the fridge for 15 minutes. Heat 1 tablespoon of vegetable oil and sesame oil in a wok or large pan over medium-high heat.
2. Remove the prawns from the marinade; cook and stir in the hot oil until opaque, about 2 minutes per side. Put the prawns on a plate.
3. Heat 1 tablespoon of vegetable oil with the oil remaining in the wok. Cook the bell pepper, pumpkin, broccoli, onion, carrot, orange peel and cayenne pepper in the hot oil and stir until the vegetables are soft, about 5 minutes.
4. Return the prawns to the pan, stir into the vegetable mixture and continue cooking for another minute. Serve over cooked rice.

Basil Chicken Stir-fry

Prep time: 10 minutes | Cook time: 15 minutes | Serves 6

- 1 tablespoon of soy sauce
- 2 tablespoons of water
- 1 tablespoon of white sugar
- 900 g skin and boneless chicken breast halves, cut into small pieces
- 1 tablespoon of vegetable oil
- 5 sliced green onions
- 3 cloves of chopped garlic
- 3 tablespoons of vegetable oil
- 2 sachets of fresh baby spinach leaves
- 1 cup thinly sliced fresh basil

1. Mix the soy sauce, water and sugar in a bowl. Marinate the chicken in the soy sauce mixture for 30 minutes. Heat 1 tablespoon of oil in a large pan or wok over medium heat.
2. Cook green onions in oil for 1 minute and stir. Add garlic and cook for 1 minute, stirring. Put in a small bowl.
3. Pour 3 tablespoons of oil into the pan. Boil and stir and marinate the chicken until the chicken is no longer pink in the center and the juice turns clear, about 5 minutes.
4. Cover and stir occasionally for 4 minutes. Stir green onion mixture into chicken and spinach; cook to reheat the onions, 1 to 2 minutes.
5. Stir in basil and cook until heated, 1 to 2 minutes. Serve!.

Mushrooms with Baby Corn Stir-fry

Prep time: 10 minutes | Cook time: 15 minutes | Serves 4

- 2 tablespoons of cooking oil
- 3 cloves of chopped garlic
- 1 onion, diced 8 sliced baby corn on the cob
- 350 g fresh mushrooms, sliced
- 1 tablespoon of fish sauce
- 1 tablespoon of light soy sauce
- 1 tablespoon of oyster sauce
- 2 teaspoons of cornstarch
- 3 tablespoons of water
- 1 sliced red chili pepper
- 1/4 cup chopped fresh coriander

1. Heat the oil in a large pan or wok over medium heat; let the garlic brown in the hot oil for 5 to 7 minutes.
2. Add the onion and baby corn and cook for 5 to 7 minutes until the onion is translucent. Add the mushrooms to the mixture and cook for about 2 minutes, until they are slightly softened.
3. Whisk the cornstarch and water in a small bowl until the corn starch has dissolved in the water; Pour into the mushroom mixture. Cook and stir until thickened and shiny.
4. Place on a serving platter; Garnish with the chili pepper and coriander for serving.

Singapore Beef Stir-fry

Prep time: 15 minutes | Cook time: 20 minutes | Serves 4

- 6 green onions, green and white parts chopped and separated
- 1 red chili pepper (finely chopped)
- 1 green chili pepper (finely chopped)
- 2 cloves of garlic (chopped)
- 3 tablespoons of dark soy sauce
- 4 tablespoons of walnut oil, divided
- 1 teaspoon of dark brown sugar
- 450 gr. Beef sirloin steak (cut into thin strips
- 400 g dried Chinese egg noodles
- 1 (280 gr. Packet of frozen minced spinach (thawed and drained
- 1 red pepper, chopped
- 1 cup of halved snow peas
- 3/4 cup baby corn cut in half
- 1 teaspoon soy sauce (divided or to taste)
- 2 tablespoons of sesame seeds

1. Mix white pieces of green onion, red chili pepper, green chili pepper, and garlic in a large bowl. Add dark soy sauce, 3 tablespoons of walnut oil, and brown sugar; Mix the marinade well. Put the beef in the marinade, cover and place in the refrigerator for at least 15 minutes to 24 hours and bring a large saucepan of salted water to a boil.
2. Add egg noodles; Cook for 2 to 3 minutes, until tender but still firm. Drain the spinach and cook in a separate saucepan with boiling, lightly salted water for 3 to 5 minutes until wilted. Drain and set aside, heat 1 teaspoon of walnut oil in a wok. Add the green parts of the green onions, bell peppers, snow peas, baby corn and 1/2 teaspoon soy sauce.
3. Fry for 2 to 3 minutes, stirring, until lightly browned but still crispy. Take the noodles, 1 teaspoon of oil and 1/2 teaspoon of soy sauce out of the wok and fry them in the same wok for 1 to 2 minutes until crispy. Put on a plate. Heat 1 teaspoon of oil in a wok and fry the marinated beef and some of the sesame seeds in portions while stirring until they are completely cooked (3 to 4 minutes. Return the cooked vegetables to the wok and sauté them, stirring, until heated for about 2 minutes. Place a light layer of drained spinach over the pasta and pour over the Stir-frymixture.

Zucchini with Lamb Stir-fry
Prep time: 10 minutes | Cook time: 15 minutes | Serves 4

- 450 gr. of ground lamb
- 4 tablespoons of soy sauce
- 1 tablespoon of chopped fresh ginger
- 1 tablespoon of chopped garlic
- 2 teaspoons plus 2 tablespoons of cornstarch
- 1 cup of canned low-salt chicken stock
- 2 tablespoons of fresh lemon juice
- 2 teaspoons of garlic and chili sauce
- 3 tablespoons of vegetable oil
- 2 tablespoons of oriental sesame oil
- 3 large cloves of peeled garlic
- 600 g zucchini (cut into strips)

1. Mix the lamb, 2 tablespoons soy sauce, ginger, minced garlic and 2 teaspoons cornstarch in a large bowl. Mix the broth, lemon juice, chili sauce and the remaining 2 tablespoons of soy sauce and 2 tablespoons of cornstarch in a small bowl.
2. Heat both oils in a wok or in a Dutch oven over high heat. Add 3 cloves of garlic; Cook for about 2 minutes until golden brown.
3. Discard the garlic. Add the zucchini and onion; Fry while stirring until they are crispy and tender, about 3 minutes.
4. Add green onions. Fry, stirring, until wilted, about 1 minute. Put the vegetables on a plate. Put the lamb mixture in the wok; Fry, stirring, until the meat is brown, about 3 minutes.
5. Add the stock mixture; Cook, stirring constantly, until the sauce becomes thick, about 1 minute. Return the vegetables to the wok; Keep frying, stirring constantly, until the sauce is heated.
6. Season with salt and pepper. Serve with rice.

Grapes Stir-fry
Prep time: 15 minutes | Cook time: 10 minutes | Serves 4

- 1 tablespoon of vegetable oil
- 1 cup of red grapes sliced
- 1 cup cooked chicken cut into cubes
- 2 cups of cooked rice
- 1/4 cup chicken broth

1. Heat the vegetable oil in a wok or large pan over medium heat. Stir in the grapes and chicken; cook and stir until chicken is hot and grapes are tender, about 3 minutes.
2. Add rice and chicken broth; continue to cook until the rice is hot, about 2 minutes more.

Shanghai Bok Choy with Ginger Stir-fry
Prep time: 20 minutes | Cook time: 20 minutes | Serves 4

- 1 piece of ginger, peeled
- 350 g Shanghai Bok Choy or other baby bok choy (5 to 8 heads)
- 1/4 cup of chicken broth with reduced sodium content
- 1 teaspoon of Chinese rice wine (preferably Shaoxing or semi-dry sherry
- 1 teaspoon soy sauce
- 1/2 teaspoon cornstarch
- 1/2 teaspoon of salt
- 1/4 teaspoon of sugar 1 tablespoon of vegetable oil
- 1/2 teaspoon Asian sesame oil
- Serving: white rice

1. Cut half of the ginger into very fine matches (about 1 tablespoon and reserve them. Grate the remaining ginger and squeeze the pulp with your fingers to obtain 1 teaspoon of liquid, then discard the pulp and remove the bruised or withered outer leaves from the bok choy.
2. Cut a bit off the end of each bok choy, then cut each head into quarters. Wash the bok choy with cold water, changing it several times, and dry it in a colander or salad spinner until it feels dry to the touch.
3. Whisk the ginger juice, chicken broth, rice wine, soy sauce, cornstarch, salt and sugar in a small bowl until the cornstarch has dissolved.
4. Wok it over high heat until a bead of water evaporates within 1 to 2 seconds of contact. Pour oil on the wok side, then swirl oil and tilt the wok to coat the sides.
5. Add ginger matches and Stir-fryfor 5 seconds. Add the bok choy and Stir-fryuntil the leaves are light green and just limp (1 to 2 minutes.
6. Mix the stock mixture, then add to the wok and fry while stirring until the vegetables are crispy and tender and the sauce has thickened slightly, about 1 minute.
7. Remove from heat and drizzle with sesame oil, then stir to brush.

Classic Chicken Stir-fry
Prep time: 15 minutes | Cook time: 30 minutes | Serves 4

- 4 cups of water
- 1/4 teaspoon salt
- 2 tablespoons of butter
- 3 dried red chilies, broken into several pieces
- 2 cups of uncooked white rice
- 1 tablespoon of sesame oil
- 2 cloves of chopped garlic
- 2 tablespoons of soy sauce, divided
- 1 skin and bone half of chicken breast (diced)
- 1 teaspoon of dried basil
- 1 teaspoon of ground white pepper
- 1/2 teaspoon dry ground mustard
- 1 pinch of ground turmeric
- 1 tablespoon of butter
- 1 1/2 cups broccoli florets
- 1 cup of diced green pepper
- 1 cup of diced red pepper
- 1/2 cup diced onion
- 1 teaspoon lemon juice

1. Mix water, salt, 2 tablespoons butter and red chili peppers in a saucepan over medium to high heat. Bring rice to the boil, cover, stir in and reduce to medium heat. Cook until rice is soft, 15 to 20 minutes, stirring occasionally.
2. Heat sesame oil in a pan or heat in a wok over medium heat. Cook the chicken, basil, white pepper, dry mustard and turmeric with garlic and stir until the chicken is browned, no longer pink in the center and the juice is clear, 5 to 8 minutes.
3. Boil 1 tablespoon of butter with broccoli, green pepper, red pepper and onion in a separate pan and stir until soft, about 10 minutes.
4. Cook 1 tablespoon of butter with broccoli, green pepper, red pepper and onion in a separate pan and stir until soft, about 10 minutes. Mix the lemon juice with the vegetables and mix the vegetables with the chicken.

Beef Lo Mein Stir-fry
Prep time: 15 minutes | Cook time: 25 minutes | Serves 4

- 225 gr. Pack of spaghetti
- 1 teaspoon of dark sesame oil
- 1 tablespoon of peanut oil
- 4 cloves of chopped garlic
- 1 tablespoon of chopped fresh ginger root
- 4 cups of mixed vegetables
- 450 g flank steak, thinly sliced
- 3 tablespoons of reduced sodium soy sauce
- 2 tablespoons of brown sugar
- 1 tablespoon of oyster sauce
- 1 tablespoon of Asian chili pepper paste with garlic

1. Bring a large saucepan of lightly salted water to a boil. Cook the spaghetti in boiling water for about 12 minutes until cooked but firm to the bite, drain and transfer to a large bowl.
2. Drizzle the sesame oil over the spaghetti; swivel to coat. Heat peanut oil in a wok or large pan over medium-high heat. Cook the garlic and ginger in hot oil and stir until fragrant, about 30 seconds.
3. Put mixed vegetables in the pan; cook and stir until slightly soft, about 3 minutes. Mix the soy sauce, brown sugar, oyster sauce and chili pepper paste in a small bowl and pour over the spaghetti until the beef is cooked through (approx. 5 minutes.
4. Put the spaghetti and sauce mixture in the wok along with the vegetables and steak; cook and stir until the spaghetti is hot, about 2 to 3 minutes.

Beef Stir-fry
Prep time: 15 minutes | Cook time: 25 minutes | Serves 4

- 1 tablespoon of soy sauce
- 1 tablespoon rice vinegar (not seasoned)
- 2 teaspoons of oyster sauce
- 1 tablespoon of cornstarch
- 450 g flank steak
- 3 tablespoons of vegetable oil
- 3 cloves of garlic (crushed)
- 1 piece of peeled ginger (sliced)
- 450 g. Chinese cabbage, leaves and stems separated as desired, then cut into pieces

1. Mix the soy sauce, vinegar, oyster sauce and cornstarch. Pat the steak dry, then cut in half lengthways and slice across. Mix with 1/2 teaspoon salt and 1 teaspoon pepper.
2. Woke over high heat until a drop of water evaporates immediately. Add 2 tablespoons of vegetable oil and stir together, then fry the garlic and ginger while stirring until they are golden brown and fragrant, about 30 seconds.
3. Add the beef and quickly spread the pieces in 1 layer on the bottom and sides of the wok. Cook undisturbed for 2 minutes then Stir-fry until the meat is browned but is still pink in the middle, about 1 minute. Place in a bowl, wipe the wok clean, then stir in the rest of the tablespoon oil and Stir-fry the cabbage stalks over high heat until crispy, about 2 minutes.
4. Add cabbage leaves and beef with juice, then stir in soy mixture and add. Fry and stir until sauce simmer and thicken slightly, 1 to 2 minutes. Discard ginger if desired; season with salt.

Melon Bean Sauce Beef Stir-fry

Prep time: 20 minutes | Cook time: 15 minutes | Serves 4

- Ice cubes
- 1 bitter melon (pitted and sliced)
- 2 teaspoons of soy sauce
- 2 teaspoons of cornstarch
- 4 teaspoons of baking powder
- 170 g beef (sliced)
- 1 tablespoon of oil
- 1/2 onion, sliced
- 2 cloves of garlic
- 1 tablespoon of chopped fresh ginger
- 1 tablespoon black bean sauce
- 1 tablespoon of oyster sauce
- 1 pinch of white sugar, or to taste
- 3/4 cup of water
- 1 teaspoon of water salt to taste

1. Fill a bowl with ice; add enough salt water to make an ice bath. Bring a large saucepan of lightly salted water to a boil. Cook the bitter melon in the boiling water for about 2 minutes until it is soft but firm; strain the melon.
2. Put the melon in the ice bath; let the melon rest until the bitter substance is extracted, about 1 hour. Drain the melon. Whisk 1 teaspoon of soy sauce, 1 teaspoon of cornstarch and baking powder together in a bowl. Add the beef and toss to make an even layer. Marinate in the refrigerator for 1 hour. Heat in a wok or large pan for 1 hour until they smoke.
3. Add 1 tablespoon of oil. Place the beef evenly on the bottom of the wok until browned, cook about 2 minutes on each side. Take out the beef. Pour 1 teaspoon of oil; let heat. Add onion, garlic and ginger; cook and stir until fragrant, about 30 seconds. Stir in the bitter melon; Cook for about 1 minute until the melon smells fragrant; Stir the black bean sauce into the melon mixture. Stir in the rest of the soy sauce, oyster sauce and sugar. Pour 3/4 cup of water; Cover and simmer until the flavors combine, 2 to 3 minutes. Uncover the remaining cornstarch and 1 teaspoon of water and stir in until thickened.

Sesame Beef Stir-fry

Prep time: 25 minutes | Cook time: 15 minutes | Serves 6

- 1/2 cup soy sauce
- 1/2 cup white sugar
- 1/3 cup rice wine vinegar
- 1/3 cup chopped garlic
- 1 tablespoon of sesame seeds
- 450 g round steak, thinly sliced
- 1/4 cup peanut oil
- 2 cups of sliced asparagus
- 1 cup of sliced fresh mushrooms, or more to taste
- 1 sweet onion, chopped
- 1 red pepper, sliced
- 1 bunch of green onions (chopped into pieces
- 1 cup of whole cashew nuts
- 1 tablespoon of sesame seeds
- 1 tablespoon corn starch (optional)
- 1 tablespoon of water (optional)
- 1 tablespoon of sesame seeds

1. Whisk the soy sauce, sugar, rice wine vinegar, garlic and 1 tablespoon of sesame seeds in a bowl; Fill in a resealable plastic bag. Add beef, coat with marinade, squeeze out excess air and seal the bag.
2. Marinate the beef in the refrigerator overnight. Heat peanut oil in a wok or large pan over medium-high heat; Boil and stir the beef and marinade until the beef is well browned, about 5 minutes.
3. Stir in asparagus, mushrooms, onion, bell pepper and spring onion; cook and stir until vegetables soften, 3 to 4 minutes. Add cashew nuts and 1 tablespoon of sesame seeds; continue to cook until the vegetables soften another 2 to 3 minutes.
4. Mix cornstarch and water in a small bowl for 2 to 3 minutes; stir into the beef and fry until the sauce has thickened, about 3 minutes. Sprinkle with the remaining 1 tablespoon of sesame seeds.

Grapes and Rice Stir-fry

Prep time: 15 minutes | Cook time: 10 minutes | Serves 4

- 1 tbsp vegetable oil
- 1 cup of sliced red grapes
- 1 cup of diced cooked chicken
- 2 cups of cooked rice
- 1/4 cup chicken broth

1. Heat the vegetable oil in a large pan or wok over medium to high heat. Add the chicken and grapes.
2. Cook for about 3 minutes until the grapes are tender and the chicken is well heated.
3. Pour in the chicken broth and rice. Keep cooking

Cashew Stir-fry

Prep time: 25 minutes | Cook time: 15 minutes | Serves 4

- 4 skinless and boned chicken breast halves, cut into bite-sized pieces
- 1 tablespoon of Cajun spice mix or to taste
- 1 1/4 cups of chicken broth
- 1 tablespoon of cornstarch
- 4 teaspoons of soy sauce
- 2 tablespoons of olive oil
- 2 cups shredded cabbage
- 25 sugar peas, chopped
- 10 small sticks of fresh asparagus, trimmed and cut into bite-sized pieces
- 3 stalks of chopped celery
- 1/2 red bell pepper, cut into thin strips
- 2 green onions, chopped
- 225 g can of bamboo shoots cut into slices (drained
- 1/2 cup cashew nuts
- 1 pinch of paprika, or to taste (optional)

1. Sprinkle the chicken pieces with Cajun seasoning. Whisk the chicken stock, cornstarch and 3 teaspoons of soy sauce in a bowl until completely mixed. Heat 1 tablespoon of olive oil in a frying pan or heat in a wok over high heat.
2. Cook the chicken in hot oil and stir for 6 to 10 minutes until it is cooked through. Remove the chicken from the pan and drain any liquids that have built up. Heat 1 tablespoon of olive oil in a pan or wok over high heat.
3. Fry the cabbage, sugar snap peas, asparagus, celery, red peppers, green onions and bamboo shoots for 1 minute while stirring. Stir in 1 teaspoon of soy sauce. Approx. Continue cooking for 3 minutes, until the vegetables are tender but still crispy, then stir the chicken into the cabbage mixture.
4. Pour the chicken stock mixture over the chicken mixture, reduce the heat to medium and cook until the sauce is thick, about 1 minute. Reduce heat to low level. Add cashew nuts and cook for 1 minute until the sauce is through. Sprinkle with paprika.

Foodie Stir-fry

Prep time: 20 minutes | Cook time: 25 minutes | Serves 4

- 1 bunch of spring onions
- 450 g skinless and boned chicken thighs
- 1/2 teaspoon of salt
- 1/4 teaspoon black pepper
- 3 tablespoons of vegetable oil
- 1 chopped red pepper
- 4 cloves of finely chopped garlic
- 1 1/2 tablespoons of finely chopped peeled fresh ginger
- 1/4 teaspoon dried hot red pepper flakes
- 3/4 cup chicken broth with reduced sodium content
- 1 1/2 tablespoons of soy sauce
- 1 1/2 teaspoons of cornstarch
- 1 teaspoon of sugar
- 1/2 cup of salted roasted whole cashew nuts

1. Chop the spring onions and separate the white and green parts. Pat the chicken dry then cut into pieces and season with salt and pepper. Heat a wok or a 30 cm pan (non-stick pan over moderate heat until a drop of water evaporates immediately.
2. Add oil and Stir-frythe chicken until it is golden brown in places and cooked for 4 to 5 minutes. Transfer to a plate with a slotted spoon. Add paprika, garlic, ginger, red pepper flakes and shallot white to the wok and Stir-fryuntil the peppers are just tender (5 to 6 minutes.
3. Mix the stock, soy sauce, cornstarch and sugar for 5 to 6 minutes, then stir into the vegetables in a wok. Reduce the heat and simmer for 1 to 2 minutes, stirring occasionally, until thickened. Stir in cashew nuts, spring onions and chicken along with the juice that has accumulated on the plate.

Chicken and Rice Noodle Stir-fry

Prep time: 15 minutes | Cook time: 20 minutes | Serves 4

- 1 large skinless and boned chicken breast, cut into bite-sized pieces
- 1 pinch of garlic powder or to taste
- 1 pinch of onion powder or to taste
- freshly ground black pepper to taste
- 225 g pack of dried rice noodles
- 4 cups of hot water or as needed
- 3 tablespoons of vegetable oil
- 4 cloves of chopped garlic
- 1 chopped onion
- 1 chopped green pepper
- 1/2 cup white cooking wine, or to taste
- 1/4 cup soy sauce, or to taste
- 2 tablespoons of teriyaki sauce, or to taste
- 160 g can of drained sweet baby corn
- 3 chopped green onions

1. Sprinkle the chicken with garlic powder, onion powder and black pepper. Soak rice noodles in a bowl of hot water until tender, about 10 minutes; Drain the pasta and cut in half with scissors.
2. Heat 1 1/2 tablespoons of vegetable oil in a wok or large pan over medium heat; Cook the garlic in the hot oil and stir in until it is fragrant, about 1 minute. Add onion and green pepper; Cook, stirring constantly, until onion and paprika are tender, about 5 minutes.
3. Add the remaining 1 1/2 tablespoons of vegetable oil; Cook the chicken and stir into the onion mixture until the chicken is no longer pink in the center (5 to 7 minutes; Stir the wine, soy sauce, and teriyaki sauce into the chicken mixture; cook until the liquid is slightly reduced (about 3 minutes.
4. Add baby corn and spring onions; Pour the sauce over evenly. Mix rice noodles into the Stir-fry-mixture; subdivide. Cook and stir until heated through, about 2 more minutes.

Appendix 1 Measurement Conversion Chart

Volume Equivalents (Dry)

US STANDARD	METRIC (APPROXIMATE)
1/8 teaspoon	0.5 mL
1/4 teaspoon	1 mL
1/2 teaspoon	2 mL
3/4 teaspoon	4 mL
1 teaspoon	5 mL
1 tablespoon	15 mL
1/4 cup	59 mL
1/2 cup	118 mL
3/4 cup	177 mL
1 cup	235 mL
2 cups	475 mL
3 cups	700 mL
4 cups	1 L

Weight Equivalents

US STANDARD	METRIC (APPROXIMATE)
1 ounce	28 g
2 ounces	57 g
5 ounces	142 g
10 ounces	284 g
15 ounces	425 g
16 ounces (1 pound)	455 g
1.5 pounds	680 g
2 pounds	907 g

Volume Equivalents (Liquid)

US STANDARD	US STANDARD (OUNCES)	METRIC (APPROXIMATE)
2 tablespoons	1 fl.oz.	30 mL
1/4 cup	2 fl.oz.	60 mL
1/2 cup	4 fl.oz.	120 mL
1 cup	8 fl.oz.	240 mL
1 1/2 cup	12 fl.oz.	355 mL
2 cups or 1 pint	16 fl.oz.	475 mL
4 cups or 1 quart	32 fl.oz.	1 L
1 gallon	128 fl.oz.	4 L

Temperatures Equivalents

FAHRENHEIT(F)	CELSIUS(C) APPROXIMATE)
225 °F	107 °C
250 °F	120 ° °C
275 °F	135 °C
300 °F	150 °C
325 °F	160 °C
350 °F	180 °C
375 °F	190 °C
400 °F	205 °C
425 °F	220 °C
450 °F	235 °C
475 °F	245 °C
500 °F	260 °C

Appendix 2 The Dirty Dozen and Clean Fifteen

The Environmental Working Group (EWG) is a nonprofit, nonpartisan organization dedicated to protecting human health and the environment Its mission is to empower people to live healthier lives in a healthier environment. This organization publishes an annual list of the twelve kinds of produce, in sequence, that have the highest amount of pesticide residue-the Dirty Dozen-as well as a list of the fifteen kinds ofproduce that have the least amount of pesticide residue-the Clean Fifteen.

THE DIRTY DOZEN

The 2016 Dirty Dozen includes the following produce. These are considered among the year's most important produce to buy organic:

Strawberries	Spinach
Apples	Tomatoes
Nectarines	Bell peppers
Peaches	Cherry tomatoes
Celery	Cucumbers
Grapes	Kale/collard greens
Cherries	Hot peppers

The Dirty Dozen list contains two additional itemskale/ collard greens and hot peppers-because they tend to contain trace levels of highly hazardous pesticides.

THE CLEAN FIFTEEN

The least critical to buy organically are the Clean Fifteen list. The following are on the 2016 list:

Avocados	Papayas
Corn	Kiw
Pineapples	Eggplant
Cabbage	Honeydew
Sweet peas	Grapefruit
Onions	Cantaloupe
Asparagus	Cauliflower
Mangos	

Some of the sweet corn sold in the United States are made from genetically engineered (GE) seedstock. Buy organic varieties of these crops to avoid GE produce.

Appendix 3 Index

JASMINE POON

Printed in Great Britain
by Amazon

19808490R00068